MW01250680

10/23/03   E NSLOW $19.95

THE
SPANISH-AMERICAN
WAR AND
TEDDY ROOSEVELT
IN AMERICAN HISTORY

The IN AMERICAN HISTORY Series

THE
SPANISH-AMERICAN
WAR AND
TEDDY ROOSEVELT
IN AMERICAN HISTORY

Tom McGowen

Enslow Publishers, Inc.

40 Industrial Road	PO Box 38
Box 398	Aldershot
Berkeley Heights, NJ 07922	Hants GU12 6BP
USA	UK

http://www.enslow.com

Library of Congress Cataloging-in-Publication Data

McGowen, Tom.
    The Spanish-American War and Teddy Roosevelt in American history /
Tom McGowen.
        p. cm. — (In American history)
    Summary: Details the pivotal role that Teddy Roosevelt played during
the Spanish-American War and the consequences of his involvement.
    Includes bibliographical references (p.) and index.
    ISBN 0-7660-1987-X
    1. Spanish American War, 1898—Juvenile literature. 2. Roosevelt,
Theodore, 1858-1919—Military leadership—Juvenile literature.
[1. Spanish American War, 1898. 2. Roosevelt, Theodore, 1858-1919.]
I. Title. II. Series.
E715.M37   2003
973.8'9—dc21
                                  2002152065

Printed in the United States of America

10 9 8 7 6 5 4 3 2 1

To Our Readers: We have done our best to make sure all Internet Addresses in
this book were active and appropriate when we went to press. However, the
author and the publisher have no control over and assume no liability for the
material available on those Internet sites or on other Web sites they may link to.
Any comments or suggestions can be sent by e-mail to comments@enslow.com or
to the address on the back cover.

Illustration Credits: Courtesy Frederic Remington Art Museum,
Ogdensburg, New York, p. 8; Courtesy William Randolph Hearst, Jr., repro-
duced from the *Dictionary of American Portraits*, published by Dover
Publications, Inc., in 1967, p. 13; Enslow Publishers, Inc., pp. 10, 34, 99,
102, 104; National Archives and Records Administration, pp. 6, 32, 55, 62,
83, 89, 94, 95, 96, 111, 113; Reproduced from the Collections of the
Library of Congress, pp. 42, 81; Reproduced from the *Dictionary of American
Portraits*, published by Dover Publications, Inc., in 1967, pp. 18, 36, 71;
Theodore Roosevelt Collection, Harvard College Library, pp. 24, 45, 69, 76,
78, 87; U.S. Naval Historical Center Photograph, pp. 21, 29, 31, 52.

Cover Illustration: National Archives and Records Administration (Bottom
horizontal photo); Theodore Roosevelt Collection, Harvard College Library
(Top horizontal and small vertical photos); U.S. Naval Historical Center
Photograph (Large vertical photo).

★ CONTENTS ★

Theodore Roosevelt (center, in dark shirt, with hands on hips) and the Rough Riders posed for this picture after the Battle of San Juan Hill. Such pictures and newspaper stories helped make Roosevelt a hero to the American people.

AN ISLAND SEEKING FREEDOM

It was July 1, 1898—a hot summer day on the island of Cuba, in the Caribbean Sea. Cannons were thudding. Cannon shells were exploding in the air with a crack, hurling clouds of bullets onto the ground. More bullets, fired from rifles, hissed through the air by the hundreds. The forces of Spain and the United States were locked in battle!

On a grassy open plain at the foot of a small hill, crouched a force of several hundred American soldiers. They were a regiment of cavalrymen—soldiers on horses—known as the Rough Riders. But they had left their horses behind and were preparing to go into battle on foot. Only one man had kept his horse by his side. He was the Rough Riders' commander, Lieutenant Colonel Theodore Roosevelt. Suddenly, a horseman came riding up to the Rough Riders. He brought an order for Roosevelt to move his regiment forward in an attack. Mounting his horse, Roosevelt rode to the head of the regiment. He began to lead his men forward.

As the Rough Riders advanced, they encountered lines of American soldiers of two infantry regiments lying down in the grass. They had not received an order to attack and did not know what to do. None of their commanding officers were with them. "Then I am the ranking officer here," Roosevelt announced, "and I give the order to charge!"[1] When they hesitated, Roosevelt angrily told them to let his men through. The Rough Riders began to pass among them. They teased the infantrymen, accusing them of being afraid to fight. Sheepishly, the infantrymen stood up and joined the movement forward.

With Roosevelt in the lead, the Rough Riders and infantrymen reached the slope of the hill and began to move upward. Everyone was walking rapidly,

Frederic Remington's famous painting Charge of the Rough Riders at San Juan Hill *shows Theodore Roosevelt in front on horseback.*

crouched over, no one running yet. To the right of the Rough Riders and infantry troops was the African-American 9th Cavalry, its men known as Buffalo Soldiers. Behind were the 1st, 3rd, 6th, and 10th Cavalry regiments. The 10th Cavalry was another African-American Buffalo Soldiers unit. The hill was soon swarming with blue-coated U.S. soldiers, led by Colonel Roosevelt. Here and there men were falling, hit by bullets as the rest of the soldiers continued forward in the noisy battlefield.

Why They Were There

Why were American soldiers fighting soldiers from Spain on a tropical island in the Caribbean Sea? What had caused this war?

Cuba is a long, narrow island surrounded by about sixteen hundred tiny islands. It lies ninety miles south of the American state of Florida. It contains about as much land as the state of Pennsylvania, and has mountains, hills, valleys, jungle forests, and grassy plains. In 1898, it was a colony of the kingdom of Spain.

Spain was a European nation that had once been a great power. But in 1898, it had a number of problems. The Spanish king, Alfonso XIII, was a twelve-year-old boy, and the country was actually run by his mother, Queen Maria Cristina. However, many Spaniards wanted a nobleman known as Don Carlos to be the king, so the danger of a civil war breaking out always loomed. Another problem was that Spain was very poor, with barely enough money in the treasury to keep the government running.

Cuba—A Land of Rebellion and Brutal Warfare

Spain still had some remnants from the days when it had been a mighty empire. It still possessed some colonies: the Philippine Islands, the Caroline Islands, the Marshall Islands, and the Mariana Islands in the Pacific Ocean, and the islands of Puerto Rico and Cuba in the Caribbean Sea.

Cuba became a possession of Spain in 1492, when Christopher Columbus landed there and claimed it for

This map shows the island of Cuba, which lies off the southern coast of Florida.

the Spanish king. Soon, Spaniards were coming to Cuba to start up farms and industries. Cuba became a Spanish colony.

People of the Ciboney and Arawak Indian tribes lived on the island, and the Spaniards forced the Indians to work for them. However, many were wiped out by diseases the Spanish brought, to which they had no resistance. With a shortage of workers, the Spanish rulers of the colony began to bring Africans to Cuba as slaves. There was intermarriage among Spaniards, the Ciboney and Arawak, and Africans.

After several generations, there were many people of mixed blood on the island. While people of unmixed blood still thought of themselves as Spaniards, the others did not think of themselves as Spaniards, Ciboney or Arawak, or Africans, but as Cubans. Some of them began to feel that Cuba should no longer belong to Spain, but should belong to Cubans.

The Spanish often treated Cubans brutally. Over the centuries, there were a number of revolts by Cubans against the Spanish. These all failed.

In 1868, a war of rebellion flared up. For ten years, soldiers of the Spanish Army fought an army of Cuban rebels who wanted to make Cuba independent, end slavery, and create their own government. The rebellion dragged to an end in 1878. The Spanish government ended slavery and promised to allow more self-government. But Cuba was still ruled by Spain— and the promises were not kept.

In the United States, sympathy existed for the Cubans for a long time. Some Americans wanted to take over Cuba and make it part of the United States. Many Cubans also favored this. Several times in the 1800s, the U.S. government offered to buy Cuba from Spain. Spain always refused.

In 1895, six Cuban men who had been living in the United States returned to Cuba. They had come to start another war for independence from Spain. The army they formed was poorly equipped, much like the American army of 1776 that fought for independence from Great Britain. Probably because of that, most Americans hoped the rebels would win.[2]

But Spain was determined to hold on to its island colony. An army of twenty thousand Spaniards was sent to battle the Cuban rebel forces. Their commander, General Valeriano Weyler, believed in using terror and harsh methods to end rebellion. The Spanish force made war on both the rebel soldiers and the Cuban people who supported them. Cuban villages were burned and hundreds of thousands of Cubans, mainly women, children, and old people, were rounded up. They were squeezed into cramped villages guarded by Spanish troops. They were poorly fed and given almost no medical care. As many as four hundred thousand people died of disease and starvation![3]

America—A Weak and Powerless Nation

All this was reported in American newspapers, which made things sound even worse than they were. There

William Randolph Hearst (pictured) was the publisher of the New York Journal. *Actor and director Orson Wells later loosely based his movie* Citizen Kane *on Hearst's life.*

were two newspapers in particular that printed such stories. These were the *New York Journal*, owned by William Randolph Hearst, and the *New York World*, owned by Joseph Pulitzer. In order to sell more papers, these two men competed against each other to print stories of terrible slaughter, torture, and brutality in Cuba. Such stories were often not true. This kind of sensational, inaccurate news reporting became known as yellow journalism. It was actually the hope of both Hearst and Pulitzer to build up such a hatred of Spain in Americans, that there would be war between the two nations. Of course, this would help sell more newspapers!

It worked. By the beginning of 1896, mostly because of yellow journalism, a real hatred for Spain had begun to grow among the American people. Many Americans now favored going to war against Spain, to help the Cuban rebels.

But it hardly seemed possible for the United States to fight a war with Spain or any other major nation. The United States was regarded by most of the world as a second-rate country, of little importance and very little power.[4] While Spain had an army of two hundred thousand men, the Army of the United States had only twenty-eight thousand soldiers. Americans just did not feel they needed a big army—it would be unnecessary and too costly to have one. The U.S. Army's main role was simply to keep peace between settlers and American Indian tribes in the western territories.

Spain also seemed to have America's Navy out-classed. The heart of the Spanish Navy was seven modern, heavily armored warships called battle cruis-ers. Spain possessed fortified bases in both the Atlantic and Pacific Oceans, where its ships could get fuel, sup-plies, and ammunition. In 1896, the U.S. Navy had only five modern-type armored battleships, and two of those were rated second class, because they were smaller. The U.S. Navy's main purpose was to guard America's coasts and harbors from any possible attack or inva-sion, should that ever happen. There were no American naval bases outside the United States. There was no need for them, because America had no foreign colonies to look after.

However, some Americans had begun to feel that America should have foreign colonies and a big army and navy. Nations that had such things were known as empires, and people who wanted their country to have an empire were called imperialists. They were also

SOURCE DOCUMENT

WE DON'T WANT TO FIGHT,
BUT BY JINGO IF WE DO,
WE'VE GOT THE MEN, WE'VE GOT THE SHIPS,
WE'VE GOT THE MONEY, TOO![5]

The term "jingoist" is derived from a London, England, music-hall ballad written during the Russo-Turkish War (1877–1878). Above are four lines from the song.

called jingoists. That term came from an exclamation American people of that time used. People would say "by jingo!" to show they really meant something.

The imperialists believed the United States had to become a great power. They felt the only way to do that would be with a war. For them, a war with Spain seemed like a good thing. And some of them, especially certain politicians, were doing everything they could to cause one!

2

THEODORE ROOSEVELT TAKES CHARGE

In the late 1800s, technology, in the form of steam engines and electricity, was creating a new way of life. For thousands of years, horses had been the only way of getting quickly from one place to another across land. Ships with sails had been the only way to travel across vast distances of water. Now, in the 1890s, trains powered by steam engines could make trips in hours that would have taken days by horse. Steam-powered ships could make voyages in days that had taken sailing ships weeks.

For thousands of years, the world had been lit only by fire—candles, or lamps that burned oil or gas. Now, electric lights had replaced gaslight in public buildings and offices of most cities. Even many ships had electric lights. Electricity had also sped up communication incredibly. The telephone was invented in 1876. By the 1890s, telephones were commonly used by offices for instant communication over short distances.

However, for communication over a really long distance, the telegraph was used. By rapidly pressing a switch on a telegraph, a trained operator could produce clicks that, when grouped together, represented letters of the alphabet. These clicks could be sent through a wire as electrical impulses that could be printed as letters by a telegraph receiver hundreds of miles away. Messages produced this way were called telegrams. Telegraph wires, strung on high poles, ran for thousands of miles across land, and ropes of twisted wires, called cables, stretched underwater from one continent to another. Messages sent by underwater cable were called cablegrams.

In the autumn of 1896, in this world of steam power and new electrical devices, a presidential election was held in the United States. Republican candidate William McKinley won. On March 4, 1897, McKinley was sworn in as president of the United States.

As all presidents do at the beginning of their term, McKinley appointed a Cabinet—a group of people to head the various departments of government. One of the most important of these departments at this time was the Department of the Navy, because the navy was undergoing changes. In 1896, the U.S. government had created a program to build a new navy. It would be a modern, technologically up-to-date navy, of armored, steam-powered, electrically lit warships such as the major nations of the world possessed.

William McKinley became the twenty-fifth president of the United States on March 4, 1897.

Warships of the 1890s—Steam, Armor, and Big Guns

The warships of that time included battleships, cruisers, torpedo boats, torpedo gunboats, and torpedo destroyer ships, usually just called destroyers. Battleships were the kings of a fleet—huge, heavily armored vessels with giant guns. The size of a warship's guns was judged by the width of the gun barrel, and battleships had either ten-inch, twelve-inch, or thirteen-inch guns that fired projectiles of the same width.

A projectile, called a shell because it was hollow and filled with gunpowder, was loaded into the breech, or bottom end, of the gun barrel. A several-hundred-pound bag of gunpowder was shoved in after it. The breech was then closed with a steel plug that locked into place. When the gun was fired, the powder bag exploded, blasting the shell out of the barrel for a distance of as much as 3.4 miles. When it hit, a fuse in the shell's nose sparked and caused the powder inside to explode.

For defense, battleships were armored against explosions of enemy shells with five inches of steel covering their sides, and eighteen inches at the waterline. A battleship was from 324 to 350 feet long and had a crew of from 350 to 470 officers and men, depending on its size. These ships could move at a top speed of about fifteen miles an hour. In 1897, the British Navy, the world's largest, had twenty-one battleships; the U.S. Navy had only six.

Cruisers were smaller, faster ships, with eight-inch or six-inch guns, and a number of smaller weapons. They ran from 270 to 402 feet in length and had a crew of from about 279 to 700 or more. Speed was from eighteen to twenty-five miles an hour. Some cruisers were armored; some, known as protected cruisers, were partly armored; some, known as unprotected cruisers, had no armor.

Torpedo boats were small, fast, unarmored ships that could speed in against a big battleship or cruiser and launch a torpedo. A torpedo is an explosive missile powered by a small engine. It rushes through the water and explodes against its target. Gunboats were bigger and better armed than a torpedo boat but were considerably slower. Destroyers were small, fast, well-armed ships designed to protect against torpedo boats.

Most warships and merchant ships of the 1890s were a mixture of the old and the new—sails and steam engines. Some still had masts and sails, like old-fashioned ships, but they also had smokestacks sticking up out of their decks. Thus, they could move with the wind in their sails, but they could move much faster when thick black smoke was belching up out of their stacks. The smoke came from the burning coal that heated water in big tanks. This created steam, which powered engines to spin propellers (called screws), driving the ship through the water.

Like many warships of the 1890s, the American cruiser U.S.S. Boston *had both masts for sails, and smokestacks for engines that burned coal to produce steam.*

America Builds a New Navy

America had launched its first armored warship, the U.S.S. *Maine*, on November 18, 1890. While the *Maine* was being built, it was called an armored cruiser. But because of its ten-inch guns, as big as those of many battleships, it was renamed a battleship second class. The *Maine* was followed by a somewhat similar ship, the *Texas*, in 1892. Still more armored ships followed.

But the U.S. Navy was doing more than just building warships. It was also working out plans to use those ships in war—particularly in war against Spain.

By 1897, the year McKinley became president, the situation between the United States and Spain over Cuba had grown worse. The possibility of war with Spain was great.

So, with all this going on, the people the president would put in charge of the Department of the Navy would have an important job. The head of each U.S. government department has the title of secretary. President McKinley appointed John D. Long as secretary of the Navy, in charge of all affairs concerning the U.S. Navy. He was a good manager and director of things, but he knew little about ships or naval warfare.

Each department has an assistant secretary. For assistant secretary of the Navy, President McKinley appointed Theodore Roosevelt. At first, McKinley was reluctant to appoint Roosevelt, but there was much powerful political support for the thirty-eight-year-old man from a wealthy New York family.

Roosevelt already had a number of significant accomplishments. He had written twenty books. These included a highly regarded history of the naval battles of the War of 1812, and several exciting books about hunting and ranching on America's western frontier. These books came from firsthand knowledge. Roosevelt had owned a ranch and lived the life of a cowboy in the Dakota Territory (now the states of North and South Dakota and parts of Montana and Wyoming).

Roosevelt also had some experience working for the government. He had been a representative in the state assembly of New York for six years. From 1889 to 1895, he was a civil service commissioner in the governments of both President Benjamin Harrison, a Republican, and President Grover Cleveland, a Democrat. As police commissioner of New York City, he had gained the reputation of being a tough, honest, honorable man.

A Man Looking for a War

Roosevelt loved ships and knew a great deal about them, and about naval warfare. He was also an eager and energetic worker. He made his typewriter's keyboard clatter as his flying fingers turned out reports, studies, and suggestions for ways to improve the Navy. In a diary, Secretary Long wrote that Roosevelt was the best man there could be for the job of assistant secretary of the Navy.[1]

But Roosevelt was a jingoist—one of the people who believed that fighting a war could help make the country greater. He firmly believed that America needed a war against an opponent such as Germany or Spain in order to gain greater respect throughout the world. In 1897, he wrote a letter to a friend who was an officer on the battleship *Maine*. Roosevelt said, "I wish there was a chance that the Maine was going to be used against some foreign power; by preference Germany— but I am not particular, and I'd even take Spain if nothing better offered."[2] To another friend he wrote, in 1897, "—I should welcome any war. The country needs one."[3]

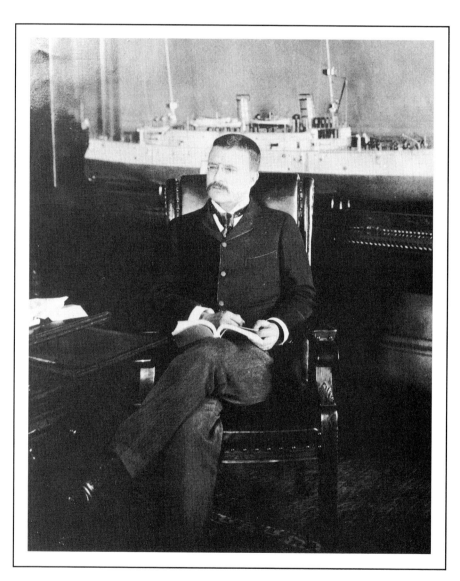

As assistant secretary of the Navy from 1896 to 1898, Theodore Roosevelt played a major part in making the U.S. Navy well-prepared for war.

On June 2, 1897, Roosevelt made a speech to the Naval War College, presenting his feelings about war. He said, "It is through strife [war] or the readiness for strife, that a nation must win greatness—"[4] In other words, he was saying that a nation could become great only through warfare.

Jingoists like Roosevelt approved of the speech. Other people, known as anti-imperialists, disliked it. Anti-imperialists believed it was wrong for a nation to use war to gain power and importance.

Roosevelt Takes Charge of Things

Roosevelt liked his boss, Secretary Long, but felt he moved too slowly and did not try to do enough to make the Navy a powerful, efficient fighting force.[5] In August 1897, Long went on a vacation, and Roosevelt was left in charge. This gave Roosevelt the chance to do some things he thought were badly needed.

Like most nations with a navy, the United States kept fleets of warships, known as squadrons, in several parts of the world. There was an Asiatic Squadron in the Far East. Roosevelt had studied the Navy's plan for a possible war with Spain and knew the Asiatic Squadron would play a very important role. It would be the Asiatic Squadron's job to attack the Spanish fleet that was kept in the Philippine Islands. But the squadron would have to be commanded by a man who was quick-thinking and tough.

Squadron commanders were replaced every few years. In September 1897, the commander of the

Asiatic Squadron was due for replacement. It was not part of Roosevelt's job to select new commanders, but he found a way to make sure that the man he wanted to command the Asiatic Squadron was appointed.

The man Roosevelt selected was a sixty-year-old commodore—a rank just below admiral—named George Dewey. Dewey was a highly experienced officer who had fought in the American Civil War. Roosevelt knew him well enough to be sure he could handle the Asiatic Squadron the right way. Dewey was also eager for the job.

Roosevelt arranged to have Dewey backed by Senator Redfield Proctor, of Vermont. Proctor convinced President McKinley that Dewey should be appointed Asiatic Squadron commander. When Secretary Long returned from his vacation, he received a message from the president, telling him to give Commodore Dewey the appointment. Long was a little annoyed, because he felt Dewey had gone over his head.[6] He apparently never knew that Roosevelt was behind it all.

By doing things behind his boss's back, Roosevelt had actually taken control of the Department of the Navy. He jokingly told a friend, "I am having immense fun running the Navy."[7]

THE DEATH OF A BATTLESHIP

A̲s 1898 began, the U.S. Navy had thirty-five ships ready for action. There were now six armored battleships—the second-class battleships *Maine* and *Texas*, and the first-class battleships *Oregon*, *Massachusetts*, *Indiana*, and *Iowa*. *Maine* and *Texas* each had four ten-inch guns, *Iowa* had four twelve-inch guns, and the others had four thirteen-inch guns. The thirteen-inch guns were the biggest ones there were. They fired eleven hundred-pound shells that could punch a hole in the armor of any battleship in the world at a range of two miles. All these big ships were also armed with eight eight-inch guns, four six-inch guns, and a number of smaller guns.

After the battleships came nineteen cruisers. Two of these were armored cruisers, their hulls and decks protected with steel armor. There were eight protected cruisers and nine all-wooden unprotected cruisers.

There were also ten gunboats, smaller than a cruiser, with smaller and fewer guns. Depending on size, a gunboat had from four to six six-inch guns and several smaller guns. Gunboats ran from 176 to 230 feet in length and could steam at speeds of thirteen to eighteen and a half miles an hour. A crew was generally about 132 men and officers. Gunboats were not armored.

Some European leaders and navy officers poked fun at the growing American Navy. They said the ships were poorly designed and badly built. They did not think the American ships could do well against a European fleet.[1]

Twelve days into 1898, rioting erupted in Havana, the capital of Cuba. The rioters were mostly Spaniards and pro-Spanish Cubans showing their anger against the idea of independence from Spain. They destroyed the offices and presses of several newspapers that seemed to favor independence. American businesses and American people in Havana were obviously in danger, because America was in favor of Cuban independence. The American consul in Cuba, Fitzhugh Lee, sent a message to President McKinley, urging that something be done to protect Americans and American property in Havana.

An Unwanted Visitor

President McKinley decided to send a battleship to Havana. On January 25, 1898, the U.S.S. *Maine* moved into Havana harbor and dropped anchor. It was believed that the presence of a warship with weapons that could rain destruction on the area would keep rioters from doing any harm to American people or property. And the sight of the big warship—with its

The U.S.S. Maine *enters Havana harbor.*

four long guns—sitting in the harbor did seem to quiet things down. There were no more riots.

But the American ship was certainly not welcome in Havana. Most people in Havana were against Cuban independence and disliked America for favoring it. When the *Maine*'s commander, Captain Charles Sigsbee, went ashore with his officers to make a customary courtesy call on the Spanish officials, they were received very politely—but very coldly. Messages accusing the United States of being a troublemaker and a bully were scrawled on the walls of many buildings.

The *Maine* continued to sit in the harbor for twenty days. On the night of the twenty-first day, February 15, the streets of Havana were decorated. It was the holiday period held before the Christian religious season called Lent. People in costume and wearing masks crowded the streets. The fun would probably have gone on well into the night, but as the clocks on Havana's public buildings clicked to 9:40 P.M., something happened that put an end to it.

A sound like a titanic burst of thunder shattered the night. In houses and buildings near the harbor, people near windows became aware of the sky brightening for a moment with a flash of light. A tremendous surge of force reached out all around the harbor. Glass in windows and doors shattered. Plaster from walls and ceilings sprayed into rooms. Ships in the harbor were rocked by the blow. Men on their decks staggered, and stared toward the source of the blast.

It was the American warship *Maine*. A tremendous explosion had blown away its front end. Its smokestacks had been knocked flat, and the deck around them was a mangled wreck. The *Maine* was on fire and sinking. All around the ship, men were struggling in the water.

Within minutes, rescue boats from Spanish and other ships in the harbor were speeding toward the *Maine*. The injured men were taken to hospitals where Spanish doctors worked earnestly to save them.

When morning dawned, the remains of the *Maine* could be seen lying in the harbor. The ship had gone down in forty feet of water. Only the superstructure, the part of the ship above the top deck still showed above the water. Parts of the ship were still burning, and a haze of smoke hung above the wreck. Of the 355 men onboard the *Maine*, 253 had perished at the time of the explosion. Seven more died later of their injuries.[2]

An Accident—Or the Act of an Enemy?

News of the *Maine*'s destruction caused shock throughout both the United States and Spain. What had caused the destruction of the warship? Only two possibilities were realistic. One was that something inside the ship had exploded. This would mean the *Maine* had been destroyed by accident. The other was that the explosion had been caused from outside the ship, probably by a mine. Mines were underwater explosive devices that floated in the water, attached by cables to heavy weights lying on the bottom. Such a mine would

The U.S.S. Maine *exploded in Havana harbor on February 15, 1898.*

explode if a ship bumped into it, blowing a hole in the ship's bottom. Some mines could also be exploded by means of an electrical charge sent from a ship or from shore. If a mine had caused the *Maine* explosion, this could mean that the *Maine* was destroyed on purpose, by an enemy!

The government of Spain realized at once that if the *Maine* had been blown up by a mine in the harbor of a Spanish colony, it could certainly mean war. The Spanish government rushed a message to the Spanish governor of Cuba. It instructed him to gather every

Only part of the wreckage of the Maine *could be seen above the water in Havana harbor.*

fact he could to prove that the *Maine* catastrophe could not be blamed on Spain.[3]

Secretary Long did not believe a mine had caused the explosion. In an announcement to the newspapers, he stated, "My candid opinion, based on the facts I have been able to secure, is that it was the result of an accident. I am firmly convinced on that point."[4]

The Hearst and Pulitzer newspapers saw the *Maine*'s destruction as a chance to create a greater hatred of Spain among their readers, which could lead to a demand for war. And so, with blaring headlines and articles filled with untrue claims, they built up the idea that the *Maine* had been deliberately destroyed by Spanish terrorists, using some type of mine. Two days after the explosion, the headline of the morning edition of Hearst's paper, the *New York Journal*, proclaimed, "The destruction of the Warship *Maine* Was the Work of an Enemy."[5] A smaller headline stated, "Assistant Secretary Roosevelt Convinced the Explosion of the War Ship Was Not an Accident." Beneath an illustration showing how a mine worked, was the caption, "Naval Officers Think the *Maine* Was Destroyed By a Spanish Mine."

Roosevelt quickly announced that what the paper had said of his opinion about the explosion was not correct. However, the paper was absolutely right. The fact was, Roosevelt did think the explosion was not an accident. In a letter he wrote to a friend several days later, he stated bluntly, "The *Maine* was sunk by an act

$50,000 REWARD.—WHO DESTROYED THE MAINE?—$50,000 REWARD.

EDITION FOR GREATER NEW YORK

NEW YORK JOURNAL
AND ADVERTISER.

The Journal will give $50,000 for information, furnished to it exclusively, that will convict the person or persons who sank the Maine.

The Journal will give $50,000 for information, furnished to it exclusively, that will convict the person or persons who sank the Maine.

NO. XXXX. Copyright 1898 by W. R. Hearst—NEW YORK, THURSDAY, FEBRUARY 17, 1898.—16 PAGES. PRICE ONE CENT

DESTRUCTION OF THE WAR SHIP MAINE WAS THE WORK OF AN ENEMY.

$50,000!
$50,000 REWARD!
For the Detection of the
Perpetrator of
the Maine Outrage!

The New York Journal hereby offers a reward of $50,000 CASH for information FURNISHED TO IT EXCLUSIVELY, which shall lead to the detection and conviction of the person, persons or government criminally responsible for the destruction in Havana of the United States war ship Maine and the loss of the lives of American sailors.

The $50,000 CASH offered for the above information is to deposit with Wells, Fargo & Co.

No one is barred, for the principle but unpublished reasons rising out a few answerable dollars by acting as a spy, or the actions of a government secret service, plotting by any devious means to revenge financial loss or cripple menacing countries.

This office may have yielded to Europe and will be made public in every capital of the Continent and in London this morning.

The Journal believes that any man who can be bought to commit murder can also be bought to betray his murders. **FOR THE PERPETRATOR OF THIS OUTRAGE HAD ACCOMPLICES.**

W. R. HEARST.

Assistant Secretary Roosevelt
Convinced the Explosion of
the War Ship Was Not
an Accident.

The Journal Offers $50,000 Reward for the Conviction of the Criminals Who Sent 258 American Sailors to Their Death. Naval Officers Unanimous That the Ship Was Destroyed on Purpose.

$50,000!
$50,000 REWARD!
For the Detection of the
Perpetrator of
the Maine Outrage!

The New York Journal hereby offers a reward of $50,000 CASH for information FURNISHED TO IT EXCLUSIVELY, which shall lead to the detection and conviction of the person, persons or government criminally responsible for the destruction in Havana of the United States war ship Maine and the loss of 258 lives of American sailors.

The $50,000 CASH offered for the above information is on deposit with Wells, Fargo & Co.

No one is barred, for the principle but unpublished reasons rising out a few answerable dollars by acting as a spy, or the actions of a government secret service, plotting by any devious means to revenge financial loss or cripple menacing countries.

This office has been cabled to Europe and will be made public in every capital of the Continent and in London this morning.

The Journal believes that any man who can be bought to commit murder can also be bought to betray his murders. **FOR THE PERPETRATOR OF THIS OUTRAGE HAD ACCOMPLICES.**

W. R. HEARST.

NAVAL OFFICERS THINK THE MAINE WAS DESTROYED BY A SPANISH MINE.

Captain-General Blanco, the Journal's special correspondent at Havana, cables that it is the secret opinion of many Spaniards in the Cuban capital that the Maine was destroyed and 258 of her men killed by means of a submarine mine, or fixed torpedo. This is the opinion of several American naval authorities. The Spaniards, it is believed, arranged to have the Maine anchored over one of the harbor mines. Wires connected the mine with a powder magazine and it is thought the explosion was caused by sending an electric current through the wire. If this can be proven, the brutal nature of the Spaniards will be shown by the fact that they waited to spring the mine until the vessel had entered the port, and the place where the mine may have been fired.

Hidden Mine or a Sunken Torpedo Believed to Have Been the Weapon Used Against the American Man-of-War---Officers and Men Tell Thrilling Stories of Being Blown Into the Air Amid a Mass of Shattered Steel and Exploding Shells---Survivors Brought to Key West Scout the Idea of Accident---Spanish Officials Protest Too Much---Our Cabinet Orders a Searching Inquiry---Journal Sends Divers to Havana to Report Upon the Condition of the Wreck.
Was the Vessel Anchored Over a Mine?

BY CAPTAIN E. L. ZALINSKI, U. S. A.

(Captain Zalinski is the inventor of the famous dynamite gun, which would be the principal factor in our coast defence in case of war.)

Assistant Secretary of the Navy Theodore Roosevelt says he is convinced that the destruction of the Maine in Havana Harbor was not an accident. The Journal offers a reward of $50,000 for exclusive evidence that will convict the person, persons or Government criminally responsible for the destruction of the American battle ship and the death of 258 of its crew.

The suspicion that the Maine was deliberately blown up grows stronger every hour. Not a single fact to the contrary has been produced.

Sigsbee, of the Maine, and Consul-General Lee both urge that public opinion be suspended until they have completed their investigation, the course of tactful men who are convinced that there has been treachery.

reports very late that Captain Sigsbee had feared some such event as a hidden mine. The English cipher code was used all day yesterday of dirty treachery on the part of the Spaniards I believe—"[6]

Roosevelt Gets the Navy Ready for War

The Department of the Navy appointed a board of inquiry, formed of eight experienced naval officers, to investigate what had happened. They talked with all of the *Maine*'s surviving crewmen, and with experts on steam engines, ammunition storage, and coal storage. None of these people believed the explosion had happened inside the ship. Divers were sent down to find the place where the explosion had torn open the ship's bottom and see what it looked like. They reported that the steel edges of the hole in the ship's armor where the explosion apparently occurred were bent inward. This seemed to clearly show that the explosion had come from the outside. That could mean only that it had been caused by a mine.

The Court of Inquiry kept all its discussions and findings secret. But there was little doubt that when they were revealed, there would be an outcry throughout America for war with Spain. Theodore Roosevelt would finally have the war he wanted.

On February 25, Secretary Long, not feeling well, took the day off. Theodore Roosevelt's second wife, Edith, was very sick, and he was desperately worried about her. (His first wife, Alice, had died during childbirth in 1884.) But he realized there was an opportunity to get the U.S. Navy prepared for war.

Theodore Roosevelt built up the American Navy while Secretary John D. Long (pictured) was out sick. Before becoming secretary, Long had been governor of Massachusetts and a United States congressman.

Roosevelt and many military experts believed that if war with Spain began, the Philippines should be seized and used as an American military and naval base. Roosevelt made sure that the Asiatic Squadron, commanded by his picked man, Commodore Dewey, would be ready and able to deal with Spanish forces in the Philippines.

The Asiatic Squadron consisted of the cruisers *Olympia* and *Boston*, the gunboat *Petrel*, and an old-fashioned and not very useful gunboat named *Monocacy*. Roosevelt sent Dewey a message that read, "Order the squadron except the *Monocacy* to Hong Kong. Keep full of coal. In event of declaration of war [with] Spain, your duty will be to see that the Spanish squadron does not leave the Asiatic coast, and then [begin] offensive operations in the Philippine Islands."[7]

Hong Kong, where Roosevelt ordered Dewey to take his ships, is a seaport on the coast of China. It is only six hundred miles from the Philippine Islands, where Roosevelt expected Dewey would have to fight. Roosevelt immediately began sending reinforcements to Hong Kong, to beef up Dewey's fleet when it arrived. He ordered a cruiser, the *Baltimore*, to pick up a load of ammunition from the naval base at San Francisco and steam straight to Hong Kong. The gunboat *Concord* was also sent with a cargo of ammunition. Another cruiser, the *Raleigh*, was ordered to Hong Kong. A small ship of the kind called a cutter, named *McCulloch*, was sent. It would be used for carrying messages between ships of the squadron. (There was no way to send radio messages between ships in 1898.)

Roosevelt went into a whirlwind of activity. He sent orders to the Navy's coal buyers to purchase huge amounts of fuel so there would be no shortage when war began. He ordered commanders of navy squadrons everywhere to take full supplies of coal aboard all their ships. He arranged for huge amounts of ammunition to be built up in places where it would be quickly available. He ordered some big guns, just sitting in a naval yard, put onto some merchant ships, turning them into temporary warships. He sent a request asking Congress to allow the enlistment of unlimited numbers of sailors.

In only one day, Theodore Roosevelt had made the U.S. Navy ready to fight a war!

AMERICA MOVES TOWARD WAR

Secretary Long was astounded and rather embarrassed when he returned to work the next day.[1] However, he saw the importance of everything Roosevelt had done, and did not change any of the orders.

As Roosevelt had indicated, Dewey's ships would need plenty of coal. They had to get to the Philippines, search for the Spanish fleet, and possibly fight a lengthy battle.

They would also need plenty of food and other supplies. Dewey took care of the coal needs by buying an entire British coal ship and its cargo of three thousand tons of coal. To take care of food and other supplies, he bought a cargo ship and filled it with supplies he bought in China. Then he waited for his reinforcements to arrive—and for war to begin. Meanwhile, he put the gun crews of all his ships on a daily training routine. This sharpened their ability to load, aim, and fire their guns as quickly and effectively as possible.

The movement toward war began to pick up speed on both sides. On March 13, the Navy Department received word that a fleet of three torpedo boats and three destroyers had left Spain for Cuba. Secretary Long began to issue orders for American ships.

The battleship *Oregon* was anchored off Seattle, Washington. The *Oregon* was a first-class battleship with thirteen-inch guns. The general feeling throughout the Navy Department was that if there was war with Spain, the *Oregon* would be needed in the Caribbean Sea. But the only way the *Oregon* could get there was by sailing south, around the bottom of South America and then up into the Atlantic Ocean. This was a long, difficult journey of about fourteen thousand miles.

There was no time to waste. Secretary Long ordered the *Oregon* to steam down the coast to the San Francisco navy yard and pick up a full load of ammunition and coal. On March 19, he sent an order to her captain to start for the Atlantic.

Five days later, Long issued an order for all the Navy's ships to be repainted. They were all wearing the peacetime colors of American warships, white hulls and brownish-yellow superstructure. Long ordered them painted dull gray, making them hard to see at a distance against a gray sea and gray sky. It was a warship's wartime color. There seemed no doubt that the Navy was certain of war.

"REMEMBER THE *MAINE*!"

On March 28, the Navy Court of Inquiry's decision on the cause of the *Maine* explosion was released to the U.S. Congress and the American public. The decision was that the *Maine* had been destroyed by an underwater mine.

To this day it is not positively known what caused the *Maine* explosion. However, in the more than one hundred years since the explosion happened, most experts have decided that it was actually caused by an undiscovered long-smoldering fire burning deep in a coal bin. This suddenly flared up, causing gunpowder stored nearby to explode.

However, it is possible that an explosive device could have been attached to the *Maine*'s hull. This might have been done by Spanish terrorists. Or, it could have been done by Cuban rebels hoping to create an incident that would cause America to declare war on Spain. But it is certain that the Spanish government had nothing to do with the explosion. Spain did not want war with the United States. It had no money, and it was already involved in a war on Cuba. An act of terrorism that was certain to cause yet more war would have been utterly foolish.[2]

However, when the decision of the Court of Inquiry was announced, Americans by the millions put the blame on Spain. A slogan created by the Hearst and Pulitzer jingoist newspapers swept the country: "Remember the *Maine*!" Many Americans, Theodore

Many American newspapers and magazines tried to stir up hatred against Spain. This cover from the magazine Judge *portrays Spain as a savage, murderous beast.*

Roosevelt among them, started to demand that the United States declare war on Spain.

The Spanish government was doing everything it could to avoid war, but it realized that preparations had to be made. The Spanish torpedo boat squadron had halted at a port in the Cape Verde Islands, directly in line with the Caribbean Sea. On April 14, it was reinforced by two Spanish armored cruisers. Commodore Dewey was also getting his reinforcements. The cruiser *Raleigh* arrived, and the gunboat *Concord*. Dewey began making his ships ready for combat. On April 19, he had them all painted gray, as ordered. That same day, the Spanish fleet in the Cape Verde Islands was reinforced by two more armored cruisers. Now a powerful force of ten Spanish warships was poised to sail to Cuba.

On the very next day, President McKinley sent the Spanish government an ultimatum—an order to do something or face certain consequences—demanding that Spain give up its claim to Cuba. Spain, of course, would not do this. On April 21, President McKinley ordered Rear Admiral William Sampson to take the North Atlantic Squadron to Cuba and blockade the port of Havana. This meant having his ships block the bay's entrance. That would keep any ships that might try to bring supplies, troops, or ammunition from getting into Havana. It would also keep any Spanish ships in the bay from getting out.

Sampson's fleet was formed of the battleships *Indiana* and *Iowa*, the armored cruiser *New York*, the protected cruiser *Cincinnati*, and five gunboats. It left Key West, Florida, at 6:30 the next morning. It arrived outside Havana at 3:00 in the afternoon and quickly moved into a blockade formation. Although an official declaration had not been made, this was a clear act of war!

Roosevelt Joins the Army

For months, Theodore Roosevelt had been telling friends that when war started, he intended to resign as assistant secretary of the Navy and join the Army. Although he loved ships and loved the Navy, he had absolutely no training as a naval officer. He would be useless aboard a ship in time of war. But he had the ability to be an Army officer. He asked the secretary of the War Department (which today is called the Defense Department) to find a place for him somewhere in the Army when war broke out.

Roosevelt felt that he had to see battle. He had been mocked by opponents for preaching about the need for war and the value of war without having ever actually been in a war. He told a friend that he felt he would lose all respect if he did not try to live up to the things he had said.[3]

On the same day Sampson sailed to Havana, President McKinley asked for one hundred twenty-five thousand volunteers to be enlisted in the Army. Some of these men would be formed into three cavalry regiments. Secretary of War Russell Alger asked Theodore

Roosevelt if he wanted to command one of those regiments, as its colonel.

A regiment of cavalry was a force of about one thousand men. Roosevelt did not think he had the experience to command a regiment. He suggested that another, more experienced man be named as colonel, and that he then be made second in command, lieutenant colonel. The man he suggested for colonel was an Army medical officer named Leonard Wood, who was President McKinley's personal doctor at the time. Wood was an experienced soldier who had seen combat in a brief war against the Apache Indians. He had

Colonel Leonard Wood (right), commander of the Rough Riders, and Lieutenant Colonel Theodore Roosevelt are pictured in San Antonio, Texas.

been awarded America's highest military decoration for bravery, the Medal of Honor. Roosevelt told Alger that Wood, a close friend of his, very much wanted to go on active duty again.

Alger agreed. Wood would be appointed colonel and Roosevelt would be his second-in-command. Roosevelt was in the Army!

War!

Spain could not ignore the American blockade of Havana. On April 24, Spain declared war on the United States.

Dewey took the Asiatic Squadron out of Hong Kong harbor the next morning. In 1898, Hong Kong was controlled by Great Britain and was filled with British warships. The British knew war had been declared and had a good idea where the Americans were headed. The British and Americans shared the same language and culture, and the British felt much closer to America than they did to Spain. As Dewey's ships began steaming out of the harbor, the crews of the British ships they passed gave them rousing cheers to show they wished the Americans luck.

However, the British did not think the Americans had much of a chance.[4] It was known that the Spaniards had seven cruisers, three gunboats, and a number of smaller ships in the Philippines. Dewey's fleet would be outnumbered. The British felt the Americans were going to their doom. "A fine set of fellows," a British naval officer said of the Americans, "but unhappily, we shall never see them again."[5] They expected the Americans to be slaughtered.

With the two ships he had purchased and the arrival of all the warships Roosevelt had sent, Dewey now had a fleet of four cruisers, two gunboats, a cutter, and two supply ships. He was confident this was enough. He took his ships to the small Chinese port of Mirs Bay, a short distance from Hong Kong, and dropped anchor. That day, April 25, the United States declared war on Spain. At about 7:00 that night, a boat from Hong Kong brought Dewey the telegram he had been expecting from the Navy Department. It said, "War has commenced between the United States and Spain. Proceed at once to the Philippine Islands. Commence operations at once, particularly against the Spanish fleet. You must capture vessels or destroy."[6]

Dewey waited one day, to get some information he needed, then set out for the Philippines on April 27. He knew there were two possible places where he might find the Spanish fleet. Both of them were bays on the coast of Luzon, northernmost of the Philippine Islands. One was Manila Bay, at the edge of which sat the large city of Manila. Fortresses with big guns overlooked the bay, and the Spaniards had made it known that the entrances to the bays were mined. Any ship coming to Manila harbor had to be guided in by a Spanish ship, following a tricky zigzag path to avoid the mines.

The other place was Subic Bay, fifty miles west of Manila Bay. The area around Subic Bay was heavily fortified, with bigger guns than those at Manila Bay. The entrance to this bay, too, was supposed to be thick with mines. Furthermore, the Spaniards would have a much better position inside Subic Bay than in Manila Bay. Thus, at either place, the American ships faced going into a mined harbor, against a bigger fleet backed up by powerful fortresses. Wherever the Spaniards were, Dewey was confronted with a very dangerous situation.

On April 29, Dewey's fleet was steaming toward Luzon. Halfway around the world, the ten-ship Spanish fleet commanded by Admiral Pascual Cervera y Topete, steamed out of the Cape Verde Islands. It headed straight west, toward Cuba.

THE BATTLE OF MANILA BAY

Dewey's fleet reached Luzon on the night of April 29. The next morning Dewey sent three ships ahead to investigate Subic Bay while the rest of the fleet followed. When the ships came together outside the bay, the report was that the Spaniards were not there.

"Now we have them!"[1] declared Dewey. He knew the Spanish fleet must be in Manila Bay.

In fact, the Spanish fleet had originally gone to Subic Bay. Its commander, Admiral Patricio Montojo y Pasarón, had looked things over there. He was shocked to find that the big guns that were supposed to be in the fortifications had never been put into place. Also, there were only five mines in the bay's entrance, not nearly enough. The admiral decided he would be better off in Manila Bay and took his fleet there.

The Spanish fleet was really not at all as powerful as it was supposed to be. The ships were all unprotected wooden ships. None had guns as powerful as the eight-inch guns of the *Olympia*, the *Baltimore*, and the *Boston*, and they were also short of ammunition. Because of Spain's poverty, the Navy was badly run down, and none of Admiral Montojo's ships was in really good condition. Only seven were actually capable of putting up a fight. The best of them, the cruiser *Reina Cristina*, had a leaky hull. The second-best ship, the *Castilla*, had sprung a serious leak on the trip from Subic Bay and had to be towed to Manila Bay. Some of the other ships were undergoing repairs and a few did not have all their guns working. The admiral felt his only chance against the Americans was to keep his ships in the bay where the guns of the fortresses could help them if the Americans came in.

Dewey had been ordered to capture or destroy the Spanish fleet. He had made up his mind to go into Manila Bay and fight a battle. In the middle of the entrance to Manila Bay lies an island called Corregidor. A ship entering the bay can go on either side of the island, through narrow stretches of water called channels. The Spaniards had supposedly put their mines in these channels. But Dewey was not at all worried about mines. He did not believe the Spanish had really mined the channels. He knew it was extremely difficult to put mines in such deep channels as these. He also knew that mines quickly lost their ability to explode in warm water such as this. He believed that the Spaniards' demand to guide foreign ships through the channels in a zigzag path was simply a trick.

An Approach Through Darkness

Dewey knew, however, that the Spaniards had a number of big guns on Corregidor and other guns at different parts of the bay. His ships would probably have to fight a gun battle with some of them, and then would have to face the Spanish fleet. To try to gain surprise, Dewey intended to enter the bay at night. He chose the eastern channel, the widest of the two.

At a little before midnight on April 30, the American ships steamed into the channel, one after another, with Dewey's flagship, the *Olympia*, in the lead. The ships moved through the channel with no lights except a single lantern at the rear of each ship, to enable the ship behind to follow it.

All the ships were in the channel before they were noticed. Then, some coal soot caught fire in the smokestack of the cutter *McCulloch*, which was last in line. A momentary burst of orange flame from the stack was seen by a Spanish lookout.

A cannon in one of the forts opened fire. The shell made a moaning, whining sound as it tore through the air between the ships. It struck in the water, throwing up a huge white splash. A miss!

Three of Dewey's ships fired back at the fort. Two more shots came from the fort, then the Spanish guns went silent. Gradually, the American ships pulled out of range.

Commodore George Dewey stands aboard the U.S.S. Olympia during the Battle of Manila Bay.

Dewey ordered a cut in speed, to less than five miles an hour. He did not want his ships to come in range of any of the forts at the far edge of the bay before daybreak. Still moving in a line, they steamed toward a distant glow of light that marked the location of the city of Manila.

As the sun rose and the roofs of Manila became visible, Dewey lifted his binoculars to his eyes, searching for the Spanish warships. He expected to see them in front of the city, but they were not there. To prevent any of the lovely old buildings of Manila from being destroyed by gunfire, Admiral Montojo had taken his fleet six miles southward. It was now in position in front of the Spanish naval base of Cavite. Dewey quickly realized this and ordered the *Olympia* to turn south. The other ships followed. Booms of cannonfire sounded from the forts protecting Manila, and a few shells whined harmlessly overhead.

After a short time, the Spanish fleet was sighted. There were seven ships in a curved formation extending out from a point of land where a number of guns were mounted. As the American ships moved forward, bursts of smoke spouted from the Spanish vessels and shells arched into the sky. But the Spanish gunners seemed to be rattled, and their aim was poor. Clearly, Dewey had caught the Spaniards by surprise.

With the American ships in a row, some five thousand yards from the Spanish line, Dewey took the binoculars from his eyes. He was in command of the entire fleet, but when battle began, each ship's captain was in command of his ship, to do whatever he felt necessary. "You may fire when you are ready, Gridley," Dewey called, giving *Olympia* Captain Charles Gridley permission to fire at will.[2] The time was 5:40 in the morning.

The Destruction of a Fleet

Gridley gave the command to fire. An eight-inch gun in the *Olympia*'s forward turret erupted in a thundering blast. A 250-pound projectile arched toward the Spanish fleet. It slammed into a Spanish ship and exploded, shattering the wooden deck. The other American cruisers opened fire. Their shells burst into enemy ships, smashing their hulls and decks and battering the superstructure. The fire of the Spanish ships was uneven and inaccurate, but the American fire was steady and well aimed. The weeks of training in Hong Kong were paying off.

Staying in line, Dewey's ships steamed back and forth in front of the Spanish formation. They moved a little closer each time they changed direction, keeping up a steady fire. Spanish captains began frantically trying to get their vessels under way, to get close enough to their enemy to cause some damage. But Dewey's fleet was raining shells down onto them, and the Spanish ships were being pounded into splinters. The *Reina Cristina* was burning furiously, with half of its four-hundred-man crew dead or injured. The *Castilla* was battered and burning, and its captain ordered his crew to abandon the ship. The captain and

This lithograph of the Battle of Manila Bay was published in 1899.

half of the crew of the *Don Antonio de Ulloa* were dead or injured, and most of the ship's guns had been destroyed. The *Marquis del Duero* had only one engine still working and only one gun able to fire. The Spanish fleet was turning into a floundering wreck! A haze of gunsmoke soon hung over everything. Dewey was unable to see how badly the Spaniards had been damaged. Captain Gridley came to inform him that ammunition was running dangerously low. Dewey gave the order for the fleet to turn away and sail out of the bay. He also ordered the ships' crews to be given breakfast. Many of the men did not want to stop fighting, but the American ships pulled back for a time.

Dewey and his officers were uncertain as to what had happened. As reports came in, they found that the ammunition was not actually as low as had been feared. Furthermore, the American ships had taken very few hits and had hardly any casualties.

At 11 A.M., the American fleet steamed back into the harbor. One of the forts fired a few shots, but return fire from American ships silenced it. The *Don Antonio de Ulloa* fired some shots, but the American cruisers slammed a few shells into the enemy ship and it began to sink.

By 12:30 P.M., the battle was clearly over. *The Don Antonio de Ulloa* and the *Reina Cristina* had both sunk. The *Castilla* had turned over and was floating upside down. The other Spanish ships lay mangled and burning in the water. It would turn out that the Spanish had about four hundred men killed and wounded, and their fleet had been destroyed. But the American ships had very little damage, and only eleven American sailors had been slightly wounded. One man had died of heat exhaustion.

A white flag, indicating surrender, had been raised over the Spanish naval base of Cavite. The American fleet sailed back and dropped anchor off the city of Manila. Manila had not surrendered, and the guns around the city were still firing occasionally. Dewey sent a message into the city, informing the governor that if they did not stop, his warships would destroy Manila with gunfire. The firing soon stopped.

Manila was linked to Hong Kong and a number of other places by cable. Dewey made a request to come into the city and send a message. The governor refused. So, Dewey had one of his ships dredge up the cable and cut it, making communication with the rest of the world impossible from Manila. The Philippine capital was now isolated and at the mercy of the American fleet's guns. Commodore Dewey had captured the Philippine Islands!

6

A SEARCH, A BLOCKADE, AND A HEROIC MISSION

On May 6, Theodore Roosevelt resigned as assistant secretary of the Navy and received his commission as a lieutenant-colonel in the Army. Most of his friends and coworkers felt he was being rather foolish. In his diary, Secretary Long wrote, "He has lost his head to this unutterable folly of deserting his post when he is of most service and running off to ride a horse—."[1]

The next day, news of Dewey's overwhelming victory reached the United States. Americans went wild. Songs were written about Dewey. Dishes and vases with his picture on them were manufactured by the thousands. Baby boys were named after him. A movement began to try to make May 1 a national holiday in his honor—Dewey Day!

He was quickly promoted to the rank of rear admiral. Theodore Roosevelt was, of course, enormously proud that his faith in Dewey had been proven correct.

Europeans were astonished over the result of the battle. It appeared as if the United States had suddenly become a major naval power, equal to Britain, France, and Germany.

During the first two weeks of May, there was concern about the Spanish fleet of four cruisers and torpedo boats and destroyers commanded by Admiral Cervera. This fleet had apparently vanished. Was it suddenly going to turn up at one of America's coastal cities, such as New York or Boston, and begin a bombardment? Or was it going to strike in some other unexpected way? The American battleship *Oregon* had rounded the bottom of South America and was now in the South Atlantic, heading up toward the Caribbean. What if Cervera was taking his fleet to head off the *Oregon* and attack it?

The Navy sent ships out looking for the Spanish fleet, but it was not in any of the places they looked. Then, suddenly, on May 12, Cervera's ships were reported in the area of the Atlantic Ocean known as the West Indies, some seven hundred miles east of Cuba. On May 15, the Spanish fleet left the West Indies and steamed into the Caribbean Sea. Once again, it seemed to disappear.

The Spanish Fleet Is Found

The U.S. Navy's commanders were now fairly sure that Cervera was headed for Cuba. But the question was, where in Cuba? Obviously he would not go to Havana, because he would run into the American fleet blockading the harbor. But Cuba is a long, narrow piece of land, with a twenty-one-thousand-mile coastline, so there were several other places for the Spanish fleet to go.

The Navy began another intense search for the Spaniards, with ships heading for several different places. But on the morning of May 19, Cervera's ships slipped into the port of Santiago de Cuba, on Cuba's southeast coast, 460 miles from Havana. The fleet now consisted of four armored cruisers and two destroyers. The other ships had been unable to finish the long voyage and had been sent back to Spain.

Cervera sent a telegram to the Spanish governor of Cuba in Havana, to let him know where the fleet was. A Cuban working in the Havana telegraph office was actually an American spy. This man learned of Cervera's message and secretly telegraphed the information to a U.S. Army Signal Corps station in Key West, Florida. Thus, the U.S. Army learned the Spanish fleet was at Santiago, and quickly informed the Navy. On May 21, the Flying (fast-moving) Squadron of two battleships, an armored cruiser, and a protected cruiser, plus the battleship *Iowa*, were sent to Santiago. This force was commanded by Commodore Winfield Scott Schley.

Cervera soon discovered that Santiago was not the best place to be. The city was surrounded by a Cuban rebel force and no one could get in or out. It was running short of food. There was not enough coal on hand for Cervera's ships to be able to fully refuel. The harbor had only a very narrow channel leading out to sea, wide enough for only one ship at a time to move through. If an American fleet blockaded the port, Cervera's force would be hopelessly trapped. He decided to leave.

However, his ships had been at sea a long time. Their boilers needed cleaning and they had used up nearly all their coal, so they had to take on as much as they could get. All this took several days.

Thus, before Cervera could get away, Schley and his ships arrived at Santiago on the night of May 27. Cervera's fleet was now helplessly bottled up, just as he had feared it might be. "We've got them now!" Schley said, much as Dewey had at Manila.[2]

A Plan to Capture the Spanish Fleet

On June 1, Admiral Sampson arrived with the armored cruiser *New York* and the battleships *Indiana*, *Massachusetts*, and *Oregon*, which had shown up at Key West on May 26. All five of America's battleships were now together, along with three cruisers and a few smaller ships. Admiral Sampson took command and spread the ships in a curving line just outside the channel entrance. At night, to make sure none of Cervera's ships tried to sneak out, American battleships moved close to the entrance and lit it up with the beams of their powerful electric searchlights.

However, Admiral Sampson was fearful that something might happen that would enable the Spaniards to get away. The hurricane season was nearly at hand, and if a sudden hurricane struck, it could drive the American ships apart. The Spanish ships might be able

Rear Admiral William T. Sampson commanded the U.S. Navy North Atlantic Squadron.

to slip out into the open sea. Sampson wanted to find a way to make it impossible for Cervera to get out of the harbor.

He hit on the idea of deliberately sinking a ship at the entrance to the channel, so that the half-submerged wreckage would prevent any ship from getting by. The American fleet had the perfect ship to use for this purpose. A coal ship named *Merrimac* was long enough to block the channel. Its engines kept breaking down, so it was not of much use.

Admiral Sampson worked out his plan with a young naval officer named Richmond Hobson, a specialist in ship design. The plan required six men plus Hobson to steer the *Merrimac* into the channel entrance and turn it sideways. Then they would blow a hole in the side with explosive charges to let water in and sink the ship. When Sampson asked for volunteers from the men of the fleet, he got enough, as he later said, "to man a hundred *Merrimacs*."[3]

In darkness at 3:00 on the morning of June 3, the *Merrimac* glided into the channel. There was now one additional man on the volunteer crew. He had wanted so much to be part of the operation that he had hidden away on the ship before it set out.

The *Merrimac* was barely into the channel when it was seen. From the shore on each side, Spanish machine guns opened fire, and bullets began to thud into the *Merrimac*'s side. Explosive shells of quick-firing guns threw up gouts of white water all around the ship. One of the shells hit, destroying the rudder. Now the ship could not be turned sideways. It began to drift into the channel. Still under fire, Hobson and his crewmen tried to set off the explosive charges, but only two went off. Slowly sinking, *Merrimac* drifted on into the harbor, well past the place where it was supposed to have sunk. The plan had not worked; the channel entrance was still open.

Admiral Sampson Requests an Invasion

Hobson and his men left the sinking ship, taking to the *Merrimac*'s life raft, which had been undamaged. In the morning, a boat full of Spanish soldiers, and with Admiral Cervera himself aboard, picked up the Americans. As he helped them aboard, the Spanish admiral praised the American sailors for their bravery. That afternoon, he sent an officer under a flag of truce to let Admiral Sampson know that all the Americans were alive and would be well treated as honored prisoners of war.

Admiral Sampson's plan had failed. Now, there was only one thing he could do to be sure that none of Cervera's ships got out of the harbor. He would have to take the American fleet into the harbor and destroy the Spanish fleet in a battle, as Dewey had done at Manila Bay. The American fleet at Santiago was certainly strong enough to do that. However, the channel leading into the harbor was full of mines, and on the hills on each side of the channel were fortresses with big guns. Sampson knew he could lose several ships on the way in. Every American ship sunk or disabled by a mine or gunfire lowered the chance for victory. The guns had to be knocked out somehow, so that ships could be sent in to sweep the mines out of the way. Only that would enable the fleet to get into the harbor without taking any losses.

On June 6, for two and a half hours, the guns of every American ship filled the air with continuous thunder. They rained shells into the harbor and onto the hills around it. Sampson wanted to see if he could possibly destroy the Spanish fleet or knock out the guns in the forts with long-range gunfire. But most of the Spanish ships could not even be seen from outside Santiago's harbor, and even though shells fell all around them, only one was damaged. Although the forts were badly pounded, not one gun was put out of action.

Sampson decided the only way he could get his fleet into the harbor without losing ships was to capture the forts and guns. But that could be done only by troops landing and attacking the forts.

Sampson sent a message to Secretary of the Navy Long. He wanted ten thousand soldiers sent to attack and capture the forts. Then, he declared, Admiral Cervera's fleet could be destroyed and the city of Santiago captured within two days.[4] Sampson was asking the Army to invade Cuba.

7

THE ARMY PREPARES TO GO TO WAR

The U.S. Navy was, as Theodore Roosevelt boasted to a friend, in good shape and ready for the war.[1] But the U.S. Army was not. It had expanded from some twenty-eight thousand men on April 23, to more than one hundred fifty thousand men by the beginning of May. However, nearly four fifths of these men were volunteers who knew very little about being a soldier. The volunteers had to be given uniforms, equipment, and weapons and taught how to use the weapons and equipment properly and efficiently. They had to be taught to understand the meaning of all commands their officers might give them. They had to be trained to instantly obey all commands, which might make the difference between life or death. To get all this teaching and training, the new soldiers had to be put into one of the Army's basic fighting organizations, a regiment.

An American infantry regiment was supposed to be made up of twelve companies of 106 common soldiers each. Each company was commanded by a captain and two lieutenants. Every four companies were grouped into formations called battalions, each commanded by a major. The regiment was commanded by a colonel, with a lieutenant colonel as second in command. A number of other officers formed a staff that assisted the colonel. Thus, an American infantry regiment was supposed to be made up of 1,319 men altogether. However, most of the regiments in 1898 had only between four hundred and five hundred men.

In May, the Army began putting its forces together for the war. In San Francisco, a small army was assembled to go across the Pacific and take control of the Philippine Islands. In Florida, an army of twenty-five thousand was being organized to make an invasion of Cuba. An army was formed by putting groups of regiments together into what were called divisions, and putting groups of divisions together into what were called corps. The force being sent to the Philippines had been termed the VIII Corps. The force in Florida was being organized as the V Corps. A corps was generally formed out of two or three infantry divisions plus a cavalry division. It also had several batteries of artillery, with four cannons to a battery. While the Army was trying to put its Cuban invasion force together, the Navy was already making its own invasion there. Forty miles east of Santiago is a small bay called Guantanamo. Admiral Sampson felt it would be a handy place for the blockade fleet to take shelter in, in the event of a hurricane, and a good, quiet place for ships to refill their coal bins. He decided to capture it.

A Spanish gunboat guarded the harbor, but it was driven off by two American cruisers. On May 10, 648 U.S. Marines were put ashore to set up a camp and defensive position. The next day, they came under "hit and run" attacks by Spanish troops and took casualties. However, a small force of Cuban rebel troops appeared and showed the Americans where to attack the Spaniards, who withdrew. Guantanamo Bay was established as an American naval base on Cuba.

Roosevelt's Rough Riders

Theodore Roosevelt was assigned to a cavalry regiment that trained in San Antonio, Texas. Roosevelt arrived there May 15. The regiment had been named the 1st United States Volunteer Cavalry. The war department had been careful to take men who were good horsemen and could easily get used to the rough life of a soldier. Most of them were westerners, many of whom had been cowboys, ranchers, or sheriffs. Some were American Indians, for whom riding a horse was a way of life. But there were men from all other parts of the country, too. They were athletes, college students, and others who had all been picked because they could ride and shoot well.

Because so many of the men were rough frontiersmen, newspapers began to refer to the regiment as "the Rough Riders." Theodore Roosevelt, often called Teddy in the newspapers (although he hated to be called that[2]), was well known to most Americans because of his work in government. Many Americans believed that it was

Lieutenant Colonel Theodore Roosevelt at work in his tent at the Rough Riders training camp in Texas.

he who had actually formed the regiment. In time, throughout America, the regiment became commonly known as Roosevelt's Rough Riders.

The Rough Riders' uniform was a dark blue flannel shirt, breeches and leggings of tan canvas, and a wide-brimmed tan hat. Colonel Leonard Wood and Roosevelt had seen to it that the regiment got the best weapons possible, of a kind they were well familiar with. The regiment was equipped with "six shooter" Colt revolvers, which were kept in a black leather holster on the right hip. It also got Krag-Jörgenson carbines—small, light rifles that fired five shots before reloading.

Lieutenant Colonel Roosevelt was in charge of teaching the men Army methods and discipline. Quickly, most of them came to realize that Theodore Roosevelt was a tough, capable, and completely fair leader they could depend on.

On May 29, the Rough Riders marched to a railroad station and climbed into trains that would take them to join the American force in Florida. The troops in Florida were assembled in and around the seaport of Tampa, a small town of twenty-six thousand people at that time. There was only one railroad track leading into it, and it had only one hotel. The hotel was reserved for the use of officers and their wives. Edith Roosevelt came there to be with her husband for a time, before he left for Cuba. Their six children stayed at home, in New York. (One of the children was from Roosevelt's first marriage, to Alice Hathaway Lee, who died in 1884.)

V Corps—Regulars, Rough Riders, Buffalo Soldiers

The V Corps was under the command of Major General William R. Shafter. Shafter had been a general in the Union (Northern) Army in the Civil War. But now he was sixty-three years old and weighed about three hundred pounds. He suffered badly from gout, a disease that causes very painful swellings in the body's joints.

Major General William Shafter was commander of the United States V Corps, which invaded Cuba.

On May 31, Shafter received the order from Secretary of War Alger to take V Corps to Cuba. Shafter instantly sent orders to his division commanders to get moving. Tampa exploded into a frenzy of activity.

The Army had purchased twenty-nine Merchant Marine cargo ships to be used as troop transports. These were anchored at Port Tampa, nine miles from Tampa itself. The regiments of V Corps were ordered to take trains to the port, with all their equipment and animals, and board the transports. They began taking down the tents they had been living in; loading their equipment, horses, and mules into boxcars; and finally piling into boxcars themselves. All this took several days.

It was now discovered that the transports could only hold about seventeen thousand men. This meant that some eight thousand would have to be left behind—along with most of the horses. General Shafter wound up taking only twenty infantry regiments, formed into two infantry divisions. For the cavalry division, he selected six regiments. One was Roosevelt's Rough Riders.

Divisions were divided into two or three smaller units called brigades. The Rough Riders were teamed up with the 1st and 10th cavalry regiments, to form one brigade. The 10th Cavalry was an all-African-American regiment that had been stationed in the western frontier territory since 1867. During that time, fourteen of its soldiers had been awarded the Medal of Honor for bravery in battles against the Cheyenne and Arapaho Indians. These tribes had fought against American settlement in their lands. The tribesmen had given the 10th Cavalry the nickname of "Buffalo Soldiers." This was probably because, with their curly black hair and great courage, they seemed like buffaloes.[3] It was a compliment. All the African-American units in the U.S. Army had become known throughout the Army as Buffalo Soldiers.

The brigade of the Rough Riders and 1st and 10th regiments was teamed with another brigade to form a cavalry division. The other brigade was made up of the 3rd, 6th, and 9th (another all African-American unit) regular cavalry regiments. However, the cavalry division would have to fight on foot, as the infantry did. The only horses that could be taken were those ridden by high-ranking officers, and those needed to pull the guns of the artillery batteries.

The cavalry division was commanded by Major General Joseph Wheeler. Wheeler had been a general in the Confederate Army in the Civil War and had been given the nickname, "Fighting Joe." He was now sixty-one years old; was only five feet, two inches tall; and weighed only 110 pounds. But he had great courage.

Confusion, Mistakes, Concerns, and Departures

The plans for getting the troops to the ships were not very well made. Everything seemed to be going wrong. In a letter to his friend Senator Henry Cabot Lodge, Theodore Roosevelt said, "No words could describe to you the confusion and lack of system and the general mismanagement of affairs here."[4] The Rough Riders had been ordered to be at the train track at midnight on June 7, to be taken to Port Tampa. The train never showed up.

At three o'clock in the morning, the regiment received an order to march to another track to board a different train. But there was no train there when they arrived.

Eventually, an empty coal train came puffing down the track, from Port Tampa. Theodore Roosevelt determined to take control of matters. With several Rough Riders, he boarded the train. He convinced the engineer to let the regiment onto the train, then back it up—all nine miles—to the port. In this way, the Rough Riders finally arrived at Port Tampa.

Everything was in confusion there, too. Thousands of soldiers were milling about while their commanders tried to find out what ship they were supposed to board.

Roosevelt and Colonel Wood finally found the officer in charge of assigning ships and got him to give their regiment a transport named *Yucatan*. While Wood went to the ship, Roosevelt ran all the way back to where his regiment waited. He led them, again running, to the pier where they could board the ship.

On June 8, the transports pulled up anchor and began to steam toward Cuba. Then, suddenly, a message arrived ordering them back to port. Some strange ships had been sighted near Cuba. Could these be Spanish ships, sent to attack the American invasion force? If so, the troop transports and all the men on them were in terrible danger. U.S. Navy ships were sent to investigate.

For five days, the soldiers, packed onto the transports, sweltered in the fierce heat of a Florida summer and wondered what was happening. At last, the Navy decided the sighting was a false alarm. On the evening of June 13, the transports again pulled up anchor and began to steam out into the sea. The invasion of Cuba was finally under way.

O_n June 20, the United States cruiser *Charleston* sailed into a harbor at an island called Guam, in the Pacific Ocean. Guam belonged to Spain, but Captain Henry Glass had orders to seize it for the United States. The sixty Spanish soldiers on Guam had not received any news from Spain for eighteen months. They did not even know that Spain

AN INVASION, A SMALL VICTORY, A BIG PLAN

and the United States were at war! They peacefully surrendered. Thus, Spain lost one of its colonies, and America gained its first island possession in the Pacific.

That same day, the invasion fleet from Florida arrived outside Santiago Bay, where the blockade fleet stood guard. Admiral Sampson met with General Shafter to plan the invasion. Sampson wanted Shafter to land his forces at each side of the entrance to Santiago Bay. Then they could move forward, attacking and capturing all the fortresses. That would enable the fleet to enter the bay without being fired on. But Shafter felt that attacks from the front on stone forts filled with soldiers and cannons would be suicidal. He

U.S. Army troops, including men of the Rough Riders, crowd the deck of the troop transport ship that will carry them from Florida to Cuba.

wanted to make the landing at a little town called Daiquiri, about fifteen miles up the coast from Santiago. It was known to be defended by only some three hundred soldiers and had no forts around it. The V Corps could probably land there without a fight. Then it could march the short distance to Santiago and attack the forts from the side and rear. Sampson agreed.

The American invasion of Cuba began on June 22. The Spanish troops in Daiquiri set fire to a few buildings and left. The American soldiers were taken ashore in lifeboats, without a shot being fired at them. Instead, they were met by ragged, poorly armed, cheering Cuban rebel soldiers who had been sent to help the invasion.

The American Army had not yet begun to wear camoflauge uniforms of brown or green that helped soldiers blend into the landscape. The troops making the invasion wore a dark blue coat with brass buttons, light-blue trousers, brown canvas leggings, and a wide-brimmed "cowboy hat" of pale olive brown. Made mostly of wool, this uniform was really too heavy for the year-round warm climate of Cuba.

The main weapon of the American infantrymen was the Krag-Jörgenson rifle. It could fire five shots, one at a time, to a distance of two miles, before having to be reloaded. However, it took a rather long time to reload.

Not enough of these rifles were available for everyone, so only the regular Army troops had them.

Volunteer regiments were armed with old Springfield Model 1873 rifles, which had to be reloaded after each shot. They, too, had a range of about two miles.

The Rough Riders Help Win a Victory

The landings went on all day and continued into the next. Meanwhile, two regiments of the 2nd Infantry Division marched seven miles through thick jungle to a town called Siboney. It was supposedly held by six hundred Spanish troops, but they, too, had left.

However, Cuban rebel soldiers brought word that the Spaniards had stopped a few miles beyond Siboney. They had dug trenches and were waiting for the Americans to walk into an ambush.

American troops travel toward San Juan.

"Fighting Joe" Wheeler rode out to look at the Spanish position and decided he wanted to push the Spaniards out of the way. He sent word back to Daiquiri, and soon the cavalry division's second brigade, which included the Rough Riders, was tramping through the jungle to Siboney.

The brigade arrived after dark. The men settled down wherever they were, made campfires, and cooked a meal—coffee; fried salt pork; and thick, hard biscuits known as hardtack. They went to sleep in the open, in a drenching tropical rainstorm.

At daybreak, June 24, the 2nd Brigade began its attack. The plan called for units of the 1st and 10th Cavalries, led by the brigade commander, Brigadier General Samuel Young, to push straight ahead. The Rough Riders, in two groups commanded by Wood and Roosevelt, were to follow a side trail and attack from the left. The total American attacking force numbered about one thousand men.

The Spanish force awaiting them was about fifteen hundred strong. The Spaniards wore lightweight wide-brimmed yellow straw hats and short jackets and long trousers of white cotton with thin vertical blue stripes. The American soldiers thought these uniforms looked like pajamas. But it was a cool, comfortable uniform for a warm climate.

The Spaniards were equipped with one of the best rifles in the world, the German Mauser. It fired five rounds much faster than the Krag-Jörgensons could. It was also much easier and quicker to reload. As the

Americans neared the Spanish position, a sudden sound began, like the popping of many corks coming out of bottles—the sound of Mauser rifles. Mixed with it was another noise, which Roosevelt later described as a "rustling sound."[1] This was the sound of bullets ripping through the air.

Americans began to fall. The Rough Riders led by Roosevelt emerged from the forest and saw a hill before them, with red-roofed houses at its top. Suddenly, a loud cheer came from the right. Roosevelt decided that must mean that Colonel Wood's group was charging. Roosevelt sprang forward, yelling for his men to follow. They swarmed up the hill toward the houses.

The Spaniards believed they were being attacked by the whole army that had landed at Daiquiri. They scrambled out of the houses and trenches and ran. The U.S. Army had won its first victory of the war, known as the Battle of Las Guasimas.

General Shafter Plans an Attack

The Spanish troops pulled back to Santiago and made preparations to fight off an American attack. The city was ringed with trenches, fences of tangled barbed wire strung in front of them. In the hills lying before the city were more lines of trenches, with as many as eight rows of barbed wire before them. A blockhouse, a fortified stone building, stood on one of the highest of these hills, called San Juan. From this blockhouse, Spanish soldiers equipped with rifles and two modern quick-firing cannons could pour fire at troops coming toward them.

Some distance in front of San Juan was a smaller hill, which was to become known as Kettle Hill, with a fortified farmhouse on its crest and more trenches. About two miles north of the hills and a mile forward of them was a village called El Caney. It was protected by a stone fort, five blockhouses, trenches, and barbed wire. There were plenty of buildings men could shoot from while hidden.

San Juan Hill, which stood in front of the city of Santiago, had fortifications and trenches full of Spanish troops along its top.

The Spanish position was strong, but there were only about twelve hundred men spread out around San Juan Hill.

Five hundred twenty men were in the trenches and blockhouses of El Caney. However, reinforcements of thirty-six hundred men were coming from the town of Manzanillo, only forty-five miles away.

American troops were still landing at Daiquiri and Siboney. The landings were completed on June 29. The next day, the entire V Corps started marching through a jungle of palm trees toward Santiago.

General Shafter went ahead to look things over, and decided on a simple plan. Together, the 1st Division and Cavalry Division were about ten thousand men. Shafter would send them straight ahead at the Spanish defenses in front of Santiago. But he knew Spanish troops were probably in El Caney. They could come out and hit his attacking force from the side. To prevent that, he would start the battle by launching an attack on El Caney by the 2nd Division and Independent Brigade, totaling about six thousand men. It would probably take two hours to kill, wound, or capture all the troops in El Caney. So, Shafter would wait two hours, then begin the main attack. The 2nd Division would then swing around and hit the Spanish troops on the hills from the left, as the other divisions were hitting them from the front. As for the reinforcements coming to help the Spaniards, Shafter was prepared for that, too. He had a force of three

As they make their way toward Santiago, American soldiers in a trench keep an eye out for Spanish troops.

thousand Cuban rebel troops blocking the road the reinforcements were coming on.

Battle Preparations, Changes in Command

During the night, the American forces took up their positions as quietly as possible. The three brigades of the 2nd Division and the Independent Brigade formed a semicircle around El Caney. The Cavalry Division and 1st Division clustered around a little hill called El Pozo, a short distance in front of San Juan Hill. The Americans went to sleep knowing that the next day they would be fighting a major battle.

As the sky began to turn light on the morning of July 1, the American soldiers ate a quick breakfast. Bugles began to blare. The men of the 1st Division and Cavalry Division picked up their weapons and formed columns. They began to move forward along a narrow trail leading through thick jungle toward the hills.

An artillery battery clattered up the side of El Pozo. Each of the four guns of the battery was pulled by a team of six horses, in pairs. Behind them, also pulled by teams of six horses, came the big wooden ammunition chests on wheels. At the top of the hill, the battery took up its position. The guns were in a line, pointing toward San Juan Hill, with ammunition chests lined up behind them. These cannons, called Hotchkiss guns, could fire explosive shells a distance of almost two miles.

The hilltop was clustered with officers of General Shafter's staff. It was from there that the army's movements would be directed. But unforeseen problems had blossomed during the night. General Shafter was in bed with an attack of gout, and he was also suffering from heat exhaustion because of his immense weight. He was unable to walk. He had sent one of his staff officers to El Pozo Hill to keep him informed of the battle's progress. He was in contact with the officer by a special telephone, rigged up by the Army Signal Corps.

General Wheeler, the cavalry division commander, was also in his bed, suffering an attack of tropical fever. His doctor felt he was much too ill to do any fighting.

The commander of the 2nd Brigade, Brigadier General Samuel Young, had also been put out of action by tropical fever. Colonel Leonard Wood was appointed to take command of his brigade. Thus, to his delight, Theodore Roosevelt now found himself in complete command of the Rough Riders.

About a mile and a half southeast of El Caney, the four guns of an artillery battery were in line on a grassy rise of ground. At about 6:30 A.M., the battery commander received the order to open fire. The target was the stone fort in the town, which was sure to be full of Spanish soldiers. One after another, the guns erupted with a flash, a bang, and a burst of white smoke. The troops moving down the jungle trail heard them booming and knew the battle had begun.

9

A LAND BATTLE, A SEA BATTLE, AND VICTORY

At about 6:50 A.M., July 1, 1898, the infantry around El Caney began to move, firing as they raced forward. The Spaniards began to shoot back and were soon causing heavy casualties. The Americans dropped to the ground, trying to gain as much cover as they could from the tall grass and bushes. They began inching their way forward. The advance on El Caney slowed to a crawl.

By 8:00, the town still had not been reached. The men of the 2nd Division continued crawling toward it, under heavy, deadly fire. They often ran into stretches of barbed wire. Then, several men crawled along the length of the wire, snipping strands with wire cutters while the rest waited. It was an agonizingly slow advance. The ground behind the crawling men was dotted with motionless bodies.

On El Pozo Hill, General Shafter's staff officer was unaware that El Caney had not yet been taken. He decided it was time to start the assault on the hills, as

The Rough Riders exchange fire with Spanish troops on the way to Santiago.

the general had planned. He ordered the artillery on El Pozo to open up. The guns began firing, one after another, at the blockhouse on San Juan Hill. Puffs of smoke erupting on San Juan Hill showed where the shells were hitting.

Suddenly, a shrill whistling sound was heard. With a sharp crack, something exploded in the air over the American troops around El Pozo. A moment later there was another whistle and explosion. Theodore Roosevelt felt a sting of pain on his wrist, where a large welt appeared. The Spanish guns were firing back with shrapnel, hollow shells filled with several hundred bullets. When the shells exploded, the bullets were sprayed out in all directions, moving as fast as if they had been fired from a rifle. Thus, a single shell might kill and injure dozens of men. Roosevelt had been grazed by a shrapnel bullet. An inch to one side, and it would have shattered his wrist.

At 10:00, the American divisions were finally ordered forward. They moved down the jungle trail toward the little San Juan River, which was flowing along in front of the hill. When the first regiments reached the river, they found no bridge and had to wade across. This slowed their movement, and the troops coming behind them had to stop and wait. The trail became thickly crowded.

A Rain of Fire

At this moment, the Spanish soldiers in the trenches on the hills opened fire. The two guns on San Juan Hill joined in, firing shrapnel. The Spaniards knew exactly where the trail in the jungle was and fired directly at it. To make matters worse, an Army Signal Corps observation balloon was being hauled down the trail behind the foot soldiers. It was an enormous, yellow, egg-shaped rubber balloon, filled with gas. Ropes were attached to it, and a number of soldiers walked beneath it, holding the ropes to keep it from floating away. A basket hung from it, in which two officers peered out at the landscape below, on the lookout for enemy soldiers. But this huge, slow-moving object helped show the Spanish soldiers exactly where the American troops were in the jungle. Wading across

The U.S. Army Signal Corps observation balloon, hanging above the jungle in front of San Juan Hill, drew fire from Spanish soldiers on the hilltop.

the river and bunched up waiting to cross, the Americans were soon being hammered by a hail of rifle bullets and shrapnel.

At about 11:00, Roosevelt and his Rough Riders reached the river, coming under heavy fire. Crossing the river, they moved onto a grassy open plain, taking a position on the far end of the line of American troops. Rising ahead of them was Kettle Hill. They halted, waiting for the order to attack. They were still under fire, and a man would go down every few minutes, killed or wounded.

At 1:00 P.M., an officer brought Roosevelt an order to move his regiment forward and attack Kettle Hill. Joined by the 1st and 9th infantry regiments, Roosevelt and the Rough Riders began moving up the hill. Five other cavalry regiments, on foot like the Rough Riders, were also taking part in the attack.

Roosevelt was still riding his horse, Little Texas. But forty yards from the top of the hill, Roosevelt was stopped by a barbed-wire fence. He got off his horse and waited while Rough Riders tore an opening in the fence. Men swarmed through, running at a crouch toward the hilltop, Roosevelt among them.

As the Americans flooded over the crest of the hill, the Spanish soldiers scrambled out of their trenches and ran toward the rear. In each battalion of an American regiment, one man carried an American flag. These soldiers all now started jamming the flagpoles into the earth. The hilltop bristled with flags, showing that the hill had been captured by U.S. troops.

Looking to the left, Roosevelt saw the men of the 1st Division charging up San Juan Hill. He called to his men to help them by firing at the Spanish block-house and trenches on the hilltop. With this help, 1st Division troops were soon able to reach the top of the hill. Storming forward, they chased the Spanish soldiers out of the blockhouse and trenches. By 1:50 P.M., San Juan Hill, too, was in American hands.

A Costly American Victory, a Difficult Spanish Choice

The battle, which became known as the Battle of San Juan Hill, was an American victory. But it was costly. The Spanish had 591 killed and wounded; the Americans had 1,385 killed and wounded—more than twice as many as the Spanish had.[1]

It was not until five o'clock that El Caney finally fell. One hundred Spanish soldiers fled from the town, 120 surrendered, and 235 were killed or wounded.

American losses totaled 441 killed and wounded. This, too, was almost twice as many losses as the Spanish had suffered.

These casualties were very high. Ten percent of the American force had been lost in the two battles. This worried the American officers. They still had to try to capture Santiago, which was defended by thousands of Spanish troops. But another battle with losses such as these could leave the Americans outnumbered.

The American commanders did not realize that the Spanish troops in Santiago were not in the best of shape, either. With the desperate shortage of food in Santiago, the Spanish troops had been poorly fed for some time and were in bad health. Many soldiers suffered from the burning fever caused by the tropical disease malaria. Also, a serious shortage of all kinds of ammunition existed.

The mayor of Santiago was, of course, in touch with the Spanish governor in Havana by telegraph. The governor knew what conditions were like in Santiago and expected the city would soon have to surrender. If Admiral Cervera's fleet was captured along with the city, it would be a terrible, humiliating blow to Spain. The governor sent an order to Cervera to make an immediate attempt to escape, despite the risks, and bring the fleet to Havana.

Admiral Cervera had to obey the order, even though he knew it might mean the destruction of his fleet. He had believed from the beginning of the war that his ships could not win a battle against the American fleet. Now, he could show only that the Spanish Navy was willing to fight the Americans as courageously and as honorably as it could. So, at 9:30 on the morning of July 3, with all flags flying, Cervera's fleet steamed out of Santiago harbor, ready to do its best.

The six Spanish ships came out of the narrow channel in line, one after another. Cervera's flagship, the armored cruiser *Infanta Maria Teresa*, was in the lead.

As it appeared, it was instantly sighted. On an American ship a signal cannon boomed, to alert the rest of the fleet.

But the American fleet had been caught by surprise. Some of its ships were missing. A battleship and two cruisers had gone to Guantanamo for coal. Another cruiser was seven miles away, carrying Admiral Sampson to a meeting with General Shafter. Most of the ships remaining were not at full steam and would not be able to move quickly for a time.

The Sea Battle of Santiago

As each Spanish ship cleared the channel, it fired at the American vessels, then swung toward the west. The captains were all hoping to break away and steam to Havana. But Cervera's ships had never been completely cleaned up from their long voyage across the Atlantic. Their bottoms were thick with barnacles, which slowed them down. A few American ships began rushing to close in. Cervera knew his ships could not outrun them. He ordered signal flags run up the mast, telling his captains to run their ships ashore and wreck them, rather than let them be captured.

The Spanish ships hurried westward along the coast at full steam. But the battleships *Iowa* and *Texas* and the cruiser *Brooklyn* quickly caught up and moved alongside, firing. A shell struck *Infanta Maria Teresa* and burst a steam pipe, slowing it down. Another shell started a fire. The Spanish cruisers were armored, but they had a lot of woodwork and could catch fire easily.

The Spanish fleet was completely destroyed by the American fleet during the Battle of Santiago Bay.

The *Infanta* was soon blazing furiously, and it was crippled from many shell hits. Admiral Cervera turned it toward the shore and ran it aground, a fiery wreck.

The *Oregon* now had full steam up and raced to join in the fight. With forward guns blazing, it headed toward the second Spanish cruiser, *Vizcaya*. A shell explosion burst one of *Vizcaya*'s steam pipes; another blew up a boiler. Exploding shells started fires throughout the ship; one caused a huge explosion by hitting a torpedo. With burning men leaping into the water, *Vizcaya*'s captain followed Cervera's example.

He ran the ship aground, where it burned and was shattered by explosions.

The third Spanish ship in line, the *Cristobal Colón*, was the best and fastest of the Spanish fleet. It nearly got away, but the *Oregon* finally caught up to it and began firing. Rather than possibly have hundreds of his men killed and injured by the American guns, the captain of the *Cristobal Colón* signaled surrender. Then, he turned his ship toward shore and ran it aground.

The last cruiser in line, *Almirante Oquendo*, was pounded by shells from several American ships. Floundering and burning, it, too, was run onto shore.

The Spanish ship the Reina Mercedes *lay helpless off the coast of Santiago, Cuba.*

The destroyer *Furor* sank from shell fire; the *Pluton* was run aground as it was sinking. By 1:15 in the afternoon, Admiral Cervera's entire fleet was destroyed, marking the end of the Battle of Santiago. The Spanish had lost six ships, and 474 men were killed or wounded. One American sailor was killed, one was wounded, and several ships were slightly damaged. The American ships put out boats and rescued as many Spanish sailors as they could.

The War Ends

The American army had taken over the Spanish trenches on the hills and was looking down at Santiago. The

Spanish troops leave Mayagues, Puerto Rico, on August 10, 1898, to engage the American forces at Hormiguero.

Spanish troops in the starving city were on their last legs. On July 17, the city surrendered. The United States was now in control of Cuba.

On July 25, an American force of five thousand men under General Nelson A. Miles landed on Puerto Rico. Moving steadily and efficiently, the Americans wiped out all resistance by the Spanish forces in the colony. Puerto Rico was now also under U.S. control.

Spain had now lost all its colonies, most of its Navy, and much of its Army, by surrender. To continue the war was pointless. Secretly, the Spanish government conducted talks with the United States on reaching a peace agreement. On August 12, American and Spanish officials signed an agreement to stop the fighting.[2] In September, representatives of America and Spain began meeting in Paris, to work out a treaty that would officially end the war.

European nations were astonished. They had expected a long, difficult war. But the "third rate" American nation had overwhelmed the supposedly dangerous Spanish kingdom in only 111 days!

·10·

A NEW WORLD POWER ARISES

Like all wars, the Spanish-American War was costly in money and lives. The financial cost was about $400 million. The cost in American lives was 5,462 dead. But actually, only 379 men had been killed in battle.[1] All the rest died from disease, mainly yellow fever and malaria.

Most of the American soldiers were brought home from Cuba by mid-August 1898. Theodore Roosevelt found that he was being hailed as a hero throughout America.

Because Roosevelt was already well known to most Americans, newspaper reporters covering the war had written many stories about him. They praised his courage and ability as a leader. The charge up Kettle Hill, which Roosevelt led, had been an important part of the Battle of San Juan Hill. But most people believed that Roosevelt had actually led the charge up San Juan Hill, and had been the main leader of the whole battle! He was extremely popular. Many people of New York State wanted Roosevelt, a New Yorker himself, to be their governor. He agreed to run and was elected on November 8.

In Paris, on December 30, the treaty officially ending the Spanish-American War was signed. As part of the peace agreement, Spain had to give up Cuba, which became a free nation. Also, Spain had to give the islands of Guam and Puerto Rico to the United States. And it agreed to sell the Philippine Islands to the United States, for $20 million.

The United States was also doing other things to help itself. On August 12 it annexed (officially took over) the Hawaiian Islands. (At the time, Hawaii was an independent republic, not a possession of Spain.) It also claimed a small Pacific island, called Wake Island, to use as a naval base.

Thus, the United States came out of the war as a new world power. It now had possessions that could

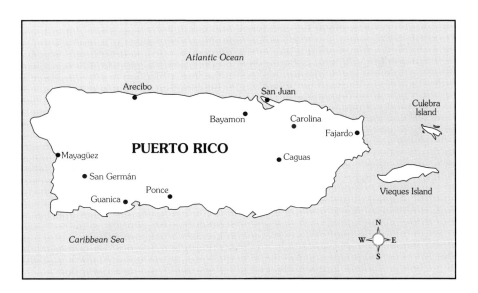

This map shows the location of Puerto Rico and some of its important cities.

become important navy and army bases in the Pacific Ocean and Caribbean Sea. Its Navy now had the world's respect, and its Army had shown a fighting spirit that had won the world's admiration.

Roosevelt served as New York governor for only two years. In 1900, President McKinley ran for re-election as president. Because Roosevelt was still tremendously popular, the Republican Party asked him to run as McKinley's vice president. He agreed. In November 1900, McKinley and Roosevelt were elected.

Roosevelt did not like being vice president. He had no real power and nothing important to do. However, less than a year after the election, on September 6, 1901, McKinley was shot by an assassin. He died on September 14. Thus, Theodore Roosevelt became the president of the United States. At the age of forty-two, he was the youngest man ever to become president.

Roosevelt Creates a Big Stick—and Uses It

One of Roosevelt's favorite sayings was, "Speak softly and carry a big stick." What he seemed to mean by this was that the United States should be peaceful and fair, but should be well able to use force, if necessary. The war with Spain had shown how important it was to have a strong Navy. One of Roosevelt's first goals as president was to continue to increase the power of the U.S. Navy. He pushed Congress to begin a program of battleship building that would increase the number of American battleships to seventeen. He wanted the Navy to be a big stick!

But it was not enough to just have a powerful fleet. Roosevelt knew the U.S. Navy needed bases in the Pacific Ocean, where ships could refuel and take on food, water, and ammunition. On the southern coast of the Hawaiian Island of Oahu, which America now owned, was a large bay called Pearl Harbor. A channel, or narrow pathway of water, ran from the bay out to the ocean. In 1902, under Roosevelt's leadership, the Navy began to turn Pearl Harbor into a huge naval base. Workers began to widen the channel so ships could sail into the bay.

In December 1902, Roosevelt had his first problem—as president—with a European nation. The South American country of Venezuela had borrowed money from Great Britain, Germany, and Italy and was refusing to pay it back. The three nations sent warships to Venezuela, to force it to pay. A German warship bombarded a Venezuelan village and put troops ashore. Venezuela, Great Britain, and Italy agreed to hold discussions to settle the problem peacefully, but Germany did not seem willing.

It seemed to Theodore Roosevelt that Germany might be intending to try to make Venezuela into a German colony. In 1823, U.S. President James Monroe created what was called the Monroe Doctrine. It was a statement that the United States would not allow a European nation to create any new colonies in the Western Hemisphere—North and South America. Acting on the Monroe Doctrine, Roosevelt sent a warning to the German emperor. The United States

Following the end of the Spanish-American War, political cartoons such as this one appeared often in newspapers. Uncle Sam towers over the western half of the world, while European leaders stare in awe.

would use force to prevent a takeover of Venezuela. Realizing this could mean war, the emperor agreed to the peaceful discussion. Roosevelt had threatened to use the power of the United States, and Germany, a major power itself, had backed down.

A New Naval Base

In 1903, the United States began leasing Guantanamo Bay from Cuba for two thousand dollars a year. That same year, Cuba and the United States signed a treaty allowing the Americans to establish a naval base at Guantanamo Bay.

Helping a Revolution

During the war with Spain, it had taken the battleship *Oregon* more than two months to get from the Atlantic Ocean to the Pacific. It was clear that there had to be a canal built to enable ships to get from one ocean to the other quickly. Roosevelt called on Congress to build a canal for the Navy.

He left it to Congress to choose where the canal would be built. Congress chose a narrow strip of land called Panama, in Central America. A canal through the land would connect the Atlantic and Pacific oceans. Panama was part of the South American country of Colombia. On January 22, 1903, an agreement was signed between Colombia and the United States. It allowed the United States to rent a six-mile-wide strip of Panama for a hundred years, and to dig a canal through it. The total rent, over the years, would come to $40 million.

However, even though the agreement had been signed, the Colombian government decided it wanted more money. It refused to accept the agreement.

President Roosevelt was furious. He considered taking the strip of Panama, known as the Canal Zone, by force. But a better way appeared. The people of Panama wanted independence from Colombia. On the evening of November 2, 1903, an American gunboat dropped anchor at a port on Panama's coast. Two days later, Panama declared that it was a new, independent nation, the Republic of Panama. Two days after that,

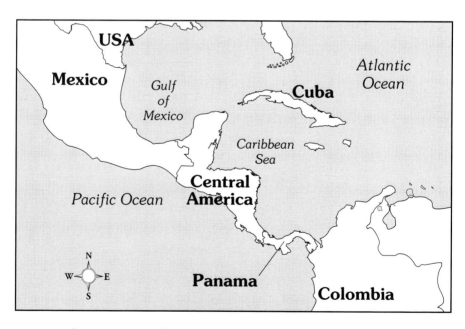

This map shows the location of Panama, the narrow strip of land that Roosevelt thought was the perfect place to build a canal to link the Atlantic and Pacific Oceans.

President Roosevelt announced that the United States accepted Panama as a new nation. The gunboat commander put troops ashore to prevent Colombia from sending soldiers to try to take Panama back. Panama soon signed a treaty with the United States, and work on the canal began in May 1904. Most Americans believed that Panama's independence had been arranged by President Roosevelt. Six years later, he admitted that it had. "I took the Canal Zone," he boasted.[2]

Adding to the Monroe Doctrine

In 1904, there was another problem between European nations and a Western Hemisphere country. Santo Domingo, now called the Dominican Republic, makes up about two thirds of the island of Hispaniola in the Caribbean Sea. In 1904, it owed money to Great Britain, France, and Germany and was refusing to pay.

President Roosevelt was afraid that the European countries might send warships again. On May 20, he made an announcement. The United States was going to see that all Western Hemisphere nations observed law and order in their dealings with other countries. In other words, America would become a kind of policeman for the Western Hemisphere. What Roosevelt had done was make an addition to the Monroe Doctrine. This became known as the Roosevelt Corollary.

Roosevelt did not do anything about the Santo Domingo problem right away. There were elections in 1904 and he was running for president, which took up a lot of time. He was overwhelmingly elected. In January 1905, he put the Roosevelt Corollary to work. The United States took charge of Santo Domingo's money problems and saw to it that the European nations were repaid.

A Prize for Peace

Early in 1904, the empires of Russia and Japan had begun fighting a war. They both wanted to become the major power in the Pacific region. Although the Japanese had soundly beaten the Russians in land and sea battles, the war dragged on.

By the summer of 1905, Russia was on the edge of a revolution and Japan was nearly out of money. Secretly, the Japanese government asked Roosevelt if he would try to arrange peace talks between the two nations.[3] Roosevelt accepted. With considerable difficulty, he got the Russian leader, called a czar, to agree to the talks.

The talks were held in America, in the city of Portsmouth, New Hampshire. They began on August 9 and went on for twenty days. Finally, on August 29, the two sides reached agreement. On September 5, they signed the Treaty of Portsmouth, and the war was finally over.

The governments of Great Britain, France, and Germany, as well as Russia and Japan, heaped praise on Roosevelt. He had gained admiration as a peacemaker and diplomat. All this was probably why, late in 1905, the German emperor asked him to settle a disagreement between Germany and France. It was a very serious disagreement that could possibly lead to an armed conflict or even full-scale war.

France was trying to take over part of the African country of Morocco, and Germany did not want to let it. The two nations were at the brink of war. Roosevelt convinced the emperor to hold a meeting with France and other European nations and talk things over. The result of this was that Germany finally gave in and let France have its way. Roosevelt had kept a war from starting.

In 1906, Roosevelt was awarded the famed Nobel Peace Prize. He was the first American ever to have received it.

The Great White Fleet

By 1907, America had sixteen first-class battleships. This gave it the second most powerful navy in the world, after Great Britain. To make the world aware of that power, Roosevelt sent all the battleships on an around-the-world cruise. They stopped at most of the world's major ports, so the ships could be seen. Because the ships were painted in the Navy's peacetime colors, with snow-white sides, they became known as "The Great White Fleet." The sight of the fleet made people all over the world realize what a powerful nation America had become.

Making America Strong Within

As well as taking the United States toward a position of world leadership, Theodore Roosevelt did many important things for the good of the nation. He destroyed a number of huge business organizations that were forcing high prices. He helped get better working conditions for employees. He tried to see that industry, farmers, and working people were all treated fairly and equally. In 1906, he pushed Congress into passing the Pure Food and Drugs Act, which has helped safeguard America's food and medicine ever since. Roosevelt was one of the first environmentalists, creating 150 national forests and 51 protected regions for birds.

A World Power

Roosevelt's term as president came to an end on March 4, 1909. By the time Roosevelt left office, the United States was one of the most important nations in the world.

WHAT ROOSEVELT LEFT TO AMERICA

Even though he was no longer president, Teddy Roosevelt was not done playing a part in America's affairs. He became more and more disappointed with the actions of the Republican president who had followed him, William Howard Taft. In 1912, he decided to run for president against Taft. The Republican Party did not nominate him, but a group of his supporters formed a new party, the Progressive Party. Roosevelt ran as a Progressive and got more votes than Taft. But the Democratic Party candidate, Woodrow Wilson, got the most votes and became president.

Back to War

World War I began in Europe in August 1914. The Allies—Great Britain, France, Russia, and Belgium— were allied against Germany and Austria. Roosevelt hoped the Allies would defeat Germany. As time went on, he began to speak out, urging that the United States join in the war against Germany. He regarded the German Empire as a danger to the world. He felt sure the United States would someday have to fight it.

Roosevelt considered running for president in 1916 but decided against it. Wilson was re-elected.

As 1917 began, it looked as if the United States was on the verge of entering the war on the side of the Allies. However, the U.S. Army was in nearly as poor shape as it had been in 1898. It numbered only 209,000 men, while the German Army was 891,000 strong. There had been many volunteer regiments, such as the Rough Riders, formed during the Spanish-American War. Roosevelt believed volunteer units were needed for this war, too. On April 10, he went to President Wilson and offered to form a volunteer division with himself in command. Once again, even at the age of fifty-nine, Theodore Roosevelt wanted to go to war.

Seven days later, America entered the war. Now, Roosevelt wanted to go to war more than ever. And, actually, the Allied leaders wanted him in the war, too.[1] He was very popular in Europe. Britain and France felt it would be good for the spirits of their soldiers if Roosevelt were in Europe as an Allied general.

But Wilson turned Roosevelt down anyway. He explained that the U.S. Army's leaders did not believe that volunteer units would be of any use. Roosevelt was enraged! He began writing columns for a newspaper, the *Kansas City Star*, in which he viciously attacked Wilson for the way he was running the war.

LOOKING OUT 7"GUN PORT
U.S.S. "PENNSYLVANIA"

Thanks to Roosevelt, the Navy was well-prepared for World War I. Above, a seven-inch gun is pictured aboard the U.S.S. Pennsylvania *during the war.*

The war ended on November 11, 1918. American forces had played a major part in making it possible for the Allies to win. America was now one of the world's leaders.

Theodore Roosevelt died of a blood clot in the heart on January 6, 1919, just about two months after the war's end. He was sixty years old.

Theodore Roosevelt's Effect on World War II

Some twenty-three years after Roosevelt's death, America became involved in another war, World War II.

For America and its allies Great Britain and the Soviet Union, this was a two-front war, with one front in Europe against the Germans and the other in the Pacific Ocean against the Japanese. Two actions that Roosevelt took when he was president played a part in helping the United States win the war in the Pacific. In 1907, at Roosevelt's request, Congress allocated $900,000 to begin turning Pearl Harbor, in Hawaii, into a naval base. In 1909, it was decided to make Pearl Harbor the main U.S. Navy base in the Pacific Ocean. It was officially opened on December 14, 1911. The first ship to steam through the channel into the harbor was the armored cruiser *California*. In a special ceremony, its prow (front) cut through a red, white, and blue ribbon stretched across the channel.

On December 7, 1941, Japanese airplanes bombed the American fleet in Pearl Harbor. A number of ships were sunk or badly damaged and about thirty-seven hundred Americans were killed or wounded, but docks and buildings were not hit. The day after, the United States declared war on Japan, thus entering World War II. Within a few days, most of America's other main bases in the Pacific—Guam, Wake Island, and the Philippines—were invaded by the Japanese.

During the war, Pearl Harbor became America's most important base. It was at Pearl Harbor that the fleets were put together and supplied for America's most desperate sea battles. At Pearl Harbor, the aircraft carrier *Yorktown*, damaged in battle, was repaired in only two days—an incredible feat. It was then able to

In 1945, sailors work to repair and clean parts on a submarine that is docked at Pearl Harbor.

go out and take part in the Battle of Midway, in which Japan's fleet was beaten and America gained the upper hand in the war in the Pacific. Without Pearl Harbor, things might have been different.

The Panama Canal opened in 1914. However, Roosevelt did not live to see the Panama Canal prove its worth throughout World War II. Ships passed through it to provide strength where needed. It was under constant guard to protect it from Japanese or German attempts to damage it. The Panama Canal was also used by the U.S. military during the Korean War and the Vietnam War.

Fighting Terror With Roosevelt's Investment

During Theodore Roosevelt's presidency, the United States established a naval base at Guantanamo Bay, Cuba. After the terrorist attacks on September 11, 2001, the United States invaded Afghanistan and drove out the ruling Taliban government and the al Qaeda terrorist organization. Many of the captured Taliban and al Qaeda were imprisoned at Guantanamo Bay.

Creating a Superpower

The Spanish-American War had seemed quick and easy. For many years it was regarded as not being of much importance. But it is now seen as one of the most significant wars of American history. It made America into a world power.

Theodore Roosevelt had a great deal to do with America's becoming a world power. As secretary of the

Navy, he truly helped make the Navy ready for war, and it was the Navy's victories during the Spanish-American War that most impressed the world.

As president, Roosevelt did a number of things that helped turn America into a major world power. By creating the second-largest navy in the world, he gave America a force that demanded respect. By actually threatening war against Germany over Venezuela, he showed that America would be fearless against any European power trying to invade the Western Hemisphere. By producing the Roosevelt Corollary, he showed that America would act as a force for law and order. By helping bring peace between Russia and Japan, he showed that America was willing to work with other nations for the good of the world.

It can be said that Theodore Roosevelt helped put the United States on the path that led it to become what it is today—a world superpower.

★ TIMELINE ★

1895—*April 14*: Leaders of a Cuban revolutionary movement land in Cuba to raise an army.

1896—*February 16*: The Spanish Army in Cuba begins a harsh program of herding Cuban people into concentration camps. American newspapers begin running anti-Spanish news stories and editorials.
November 3: William McKinley is elected president of the United States.

1897—*April 6*: McKinley nominates Theodore Roosevelt assistant secretary of the Navy.

1898—*January 12*: Rioting in Havana endangers Americans and American property.
January 25: The U.S.S. *Maine* enters Havana harbor.
February 15: The *Maine* is sunk in Havana harbor by an explosion.
February 25: Theodore Roosevelt sends out a number of orders making the Navy ready for war.
March 28: A Naval Court of Inquiry releases its finding that the *Maine* was destroyed by an underwater mine.
April 22: The U.S. North Atlantic Squadron blockades Havana harbor—an act of war.
April 24: Spain declares war on the United States.
April 25: The United States declares war on Spain.

May 1: The U.S. Asiatic Squadron, commanded by Commodore George Dewey, engages a Spanish fleet in battle in Manila Bay at the Philippine island of Luzon, and destroys it.

May 6: Theodore Roosevelt resigns as assistant secretary of the Navy and receives a commission as a lieutenant colonel in the U.S. Army.

June 22: American forces begin landing in Cuba.

June 24: The Rough Riders and other American troops win America's first land victory, the Battle of Las Guasimas, pushing Spanish troops out of the way on the advance to Santiago.

July 1: The American V Corps wins the Battle of San Juan Hill, driving Spanish forces back into Santiago.

July 3: The Spanish naval squadron of Admiral Cervera attempts to break out of Santiago harbor and is completely destroyed by the American blockading fleet.

July 17: Santiago surrenders to American forces.

July 25: American forces invade Puerto Rico.

August 12: The American and Spanish governments sign a peace agreement.

November 8: Theodore Roosevelt, a popular war hero, is elected governor of New York State.

December 10: The United States and Spain sign the Treaty of Paris, officially ending the war.

1900—*November 3*: William McKinley is re-elected president, with Theodore Roosevelt as his vice president.

1901—*September 6*: President McKinley is shot by a terrorist.
September 14: President McKinley dies. Theodore Roosevelt is sworn in as president of the United States.

1903—*November 6*: The United States officially acknowledges the new Republic of Panama, formed from a portion of the nation of Colombia, with Roosevelt's help.

1904—*February 23*: The United States signs a treaty with the Republic of Panama, which gives the United States the right to build a canal through Panama. Work on the Panama Canal begins in May.
May 20: In a letter to the secretary of war, Roosevelt proclaims what becomes known as the Roosevelt Corollary—a statement that, as a result of the Monroe Doctrine, the United States would act as an international peacekeeper in the Western Hemisphere.
November 8: Roosevelt is elected for a full term as president.

1905—*August 5*: At the request of the Japanese government, Roosevelt opens peace negotiations between the Russian Empire and the empire of Japan, to bring an end to the Russo-Japanese War.

1906—*January 16*: Having been asked by the German emperor to resolve a dispute between Germany and France, Roosevelt arranges for discussions to begin between the two nations. With Roosevelt's help, the dispute, which could have caused a major war in Europe, is eventually settled.

November 15: Theodore Roosevelt becomes the first American to receive a Nobel Peace Prize, for arranging the peace agreement that ended the Russo-Japanese War.

1907—*December 16*: Roosevelt sends the sixteen American battleships on an around-the-world cruise to show America's sea power. They become known as the Great White Fleet.

1909—*February 22*: The Great White Fleet returns from its around-the-world cruise.

March 3: Roosevelt's term as president ends.

1911—*December 14*: Pearl Harbor naval base officially opens.

1914—Panama Canal opens.

1917—*April 17*: United States enters World War I.

1918—*November 11*: World War I ends with the Allies victorious, due in part to U.S. manpower.

1919—*January 6*: Theodore Roosevelt dies at age sixty.

1941—*December 7*: Pearl Harbor bombed by Japan.

1941—Pearl Harbor remains a key naval base where
–1945 ships are repaired and supplied and fleets are
assembled before going to fight against Japan
in the Pacific; Panama Canal used to aid ship
movement during World War II.

2001—Taliban and al Qaeda prisoners are imprisoned
at Guantanamo Bay during the war on terror.

★ CHAPTER NOTES ★

Chapter 1. An Island Seeking Freedom

1. Theodore Roosevelt and Richard Bak, *The Rough Riders* (Dallas: Taylor Publishing, 1997), p. 140.

2. H. W. Brands, Jr., *T. R.: The Last Romantic* (New York: Basic Books, 1997), p. 311.

3. Kenneth Wimmel, *Theodore Roosevelt and the Great White Fleet: American Sea Power Comes of Age* (Washington and London: Brassey's, 1998), p. 98.

4. Paul Kennedy, *The Rise and Fall of the Great Powers* (New York: Random House, 1987), p. 194.

5. Warren Zimmermann, "Jingoes, Goo-Goos, and the Rise of America's Empire," *The Wilson Quarterly*, Spring 1998, <http:wwics.si.edu/OUTREACH/WQ/WQSELECT/ZIMMER.HTM> (September 19, 2002).

Chapter 2. Theodore Roosevelt Takes Charge

1. Nathan Miller, *Theodore Roosevelt, A Life* (New York: William Morrow and Company, 1992), p. 251.

2. H. W. Brands, Jr., *T. R.: The Last Romantic* (New York: Basic Books, 1997), p. 323.

3. Theodore Roosevelt and Richard Bak, *The Rough Riders* (Dallas: Taylor Publishing, 1997), p. 10.

4. Kenneth Wimmel, *Theodore Roosevelt and the Great White Fleet: American Sea Power Comes of Age* (Washington and London: Brassey's, 1998), p. 90.

5. Michael Blow, *A Ship to Remember: The* Maine *and the Spanish-American War* (New York: William Morrow and Company, 1992), p. 21.

6. G.J.A. O'Toole, *The Spanish War* (New York: W. W. Norton & Company, 1984), p. 103.

7. Ibid., p. 23.

Chapter 3. The Death of a Battleship

1. Michael Blow, *A Ship to Remember: The* Maine *and the Spanish-American War* (New York: William Morrow and Company, 1992), p. 71.

2. Donald M. Goldstein, *The Spanish-American War* (Washington and London: Brassey's, 1998), p. 12.

3. G.J.A. O'Toole, *The Spanish War* (New York: W. W. Norton & Company, 1984), p. 125.

4. The Chicago *Daily News*, Thursday, February 17, 1898, p. 1.

5. The *New York Journal*, Thursday, February 17, 1898, p. 1.

6. Blow, p. 110.

7. H. W. Brands, Jr., *T. R.: The Last Romantic* (New York: Basic Books, 1997), p. 326.

Chapter 4. America Moves Toward War

1. Michael Blow, *A Ship to Remember: The* Maine *and the Spanish-American War* (New York: William Morrow and Company, 1992), p. 122.

2. Kenneth Wimmel, *Theodore Roosevelt and the Great White Fleet: American Sea Power Comes of Age* (Washington and London: Brassey's, 1998), p. 102.

3. Ibid., p. 113.

4. Blow, pp. 183–184.

5. Wimmel, p. 117.

6. Ibid.

Chapter 5. The Battle of Manila Bay

1. Michael Blow, *A Ship to Remember: The* Maine *and the Spanish-American War* (New York: William Morrow and Company, 1992), p. 223.

2. Ibid., p. 228.

Chapter 6. A Search, a Blockade, and a Heroic Mission

1. Michael Blow, *A Ship to Remember: The* Maine *and the Spanish-American War* (New York: William Morrow and Company, Inc., 1992), p. 236.

2. Kenneth Wimmel, *Theodore Roosevelt and the Great White Fleet: American Sea Power Comes of Age* (Washington and London: Brassey's, 1998), p. 133.

3. Donald M. Goldstein, *The Spanish-American War* (Washington and London: Brassey's, 1998), p. 67.

4. Robert W. Love, Jr., *History of the U.S. Navy: Volume 1, 1775–1941* (Harrisburg, Pa.: Stackpole Books, 1992), p. 397.

Chapter 7. The Army Prepares to Go to War

1. Kenneth Wimmel, *Theodore Roosevelt and the Great White Fleet: American Sea Power Comes of Age* (Washington and London: Brassey's, 1998), p. 113.

2. Edmund Morris, *The Rise of Theodore Roosevelt* (New York: Coward, McCann & Geohagen, Inc., 1979), p. 20.

3. Theodore Roosevelt and Richard Bak, *The Rough Riders* (Dallas: Taylor Publishing, 1997), p. 172.

4. H. W. Brands, Jr., *T. R.: The Last Romantic* (New York: Basic Books, 1997), p. 345.

Chapter 8. An Invasion, a Small Victory, a Big Plan

1. Theodore Roosevelt and Richard Bak, *The Rough Riders* (Dallas: Taylor Publishing, 1997), p. 112.

Chapter 9. A Land Battle, a Sea Battle, and Victory

1. Donald M. Goldstein, *The Spanish-American War* (Washington and London: Brassey's, 1998), p. 120.

2. Michael Blow, *A Ship to Remember: The* Maine *and the Spanish-American War* (New York: William Morrow and Company, 1992), p. 382.

Chapter 10. A New World Power Arises

1. Theodore Roosevelt and Richard Bak, *The Rough Riders* (Dallas: Taylor Publishing, 1997), p. 24.

2. Robert W. Love, Jr., *History of the U.S. Navy: Volume 1, 1775–1941* (Harrisburg, Pa.: Stackpole Books, 1992), p. 424.

3. H. W. Brands, Jr., *T. R.: The Last Romantic* (New York: Basic Books, 1997), p. 533.

Chapter 11. What Roosevelt Left to America

1. Nathan Miller, *Theodore Roosevelt, A Life* (New York: William Morris and Company, Inc., 1992), p. 556.

★ FURTHER READING ★

Collins, Mary. *The Spanish American War*. New York: Children's Press, 1998.

Donnelly, Matthew. *Theodore Roosevelt: Larger Than Life*. North Haven, Conn.: Shoe String Press, 2002.

Gay, Kathlyn, and Martin Gay. *Spanish-American War*. New York: Twenty-First Century Books, 1995.

Kent, Zachary. *The Story of the Rough Riders*. Danbury, Conn.: Children's Press, 1991.

Mann, Elizabeth. *The Panama Canal: The Story of How a Jungle Was Conquered and the World Made Smaller*. New York: Mikaya Press, 1998.

Marrin, Albert. *The Spanish-American War*. New York: Atheneum Books for Young Readers, 1991.

Whitelaw, Nancy. *Theodore Roosevelt Takes Charge*. Morton Grove, Ill.: Albert Whitman, 1991.

Wukovits, John F. *The Spanish-American War*. Farmington Hills, Mich.: Gale Group, 2001.

★ INTERNET ADDRESSES ★

Theodore Roosevelt Association. n.d. <http://www. theodoreroosevelt.org>.

"The United States Becomes a World Power." *Gilder Lehrman Explorations.* September 20, 2002. <http://www.gliah.uh.edu/modules/worldpower/ index.cfm>.

"The World of 1898: The Spanish American War." *Library of Congress.* n.d. <http://www.loc.gov/rr/ hispanic/1898/>.

★ INDEX ★